#1 Teacher Recommended!

Summer Bridge
ACTIVITIES®

BRIDGING GRADES
6 to 7

Carson Dellosa Education
Greensboro, North Carolina

Caution: Exercise activities may require adult supervision. Before beginning any exercise activity, consult a physician. Written parental permission is suggested for those using this book in group situations. Children should always warm up prior to beginning any exercise activity and should stop immediately if they feel any discomfort during exercise.

Caution: Before beginning any food activity, ask parents' permission and inquire about the child's food allergies and religious or other food restrictions.

Caution: Nature activities may require adult supervision. Before beginning any nature activity, ask parents' permission and inquire about the child's plant and animal allergies. Remind the child not to touch plants or animals during the activity without adult supervision.

Caution: Before completing any balloon activity, ask parents' permission and inquire about possible latex allergies. Also, remember that uninflated or popped balloons may present a choking hazard.

The authors and publisher are not responsible or liable for any injury that may result from performing the exercises or activities in this book.

Summer Bridge®
An imprint of Carson Dellosa Education
PO Box 35665
Greensboro, NC 27425 USA

Printed in the USA • All rights reserved.   ISBN 978-1-4838-1586-2

01-119227784

Table of Contents

Making the Most of *Summer Bridge Activities*®

This book will help your child review sixth grade skills and preview seventh grade skills. Inside, find lots of resources that encourage your child to practice, learn, and grow while getting a head start on the new school year ahead.

Just 15 Minutes a Day

...is all it takes to stay sharp with learning activities for each weekday, all summer long!

Month-by-Month Organization

Three color-coded sections match the three months of summer vacation. Each month begins with a goal-setting and vocabulary-building activity. You'll also find an introduction to the section's fitness and character-building focus.

Daily Activities

Two pages of activities are provided for each weekday. They'll take about 15 minutes to complete. Activities will help your child practice these skills and more:

- Grammar and usage
- Writing
- Reading comprehension
- Vocabulary
- Algebraic expressions
- Measuring area and volume
- Geometry
- Statistics and probability

Plenty of Bonus Features

...match your child's needs and interests!

Bonus Activities

Social studies activities explore places, maps, and more—a perfect complement to summer travel. Science experiments invite your child to interact with the world and build critical thinking skills.

Take It Outside!

A collection of fun ideas for outdoor observation, exploration, learning, and play is provided for each summer month.

Special Features

FITNESS FLASH: Quick exercises to develop strength, flexibility, and fitness

CHARACTER CHECK: Ideas for developing kindness, honesty, tolerance, and more

FACTOID: Fun trivia facts

Skill-Building Flash Cards

Cut out the cards at the back of the book. Store in a zip-top bag or punch a hole in each one and thread on a ring. Take the cards along with you for practice on the go.

Certificate of Congratulations

At the end of the summer, complete and present the certificate at the back of the book. Congratulate your child for being well prepared for the next school year.

Skills Matrix

Day	Addition & Subtraction	Algebra & Ratios	Capitalization & Punctuation	Character Development	Data Analysis & Probability	Decimals & Percentages	Fitness	Fractions	Geometry & Measurement	Language Arts	Multiplication & Division	Parts of Speech	Problem Solving	Puzzles	Reading Comprehension	Science	Sentence Types & Structure	Social Studies	Usage	Writing
1	★									★	★					★				
2										★	★						★	★		
3			★					★							★					
4										★	★									★
5		★	★			★				★										
6										★					★		★			
7								★		★			★				★			
8						★				★						★				
9										★					★			★		
10		★		★						★										
11		★								★								★		
12					★					★		★								★
13		★													★		★			
14										★			★						★	★
15		★					★			★		★								
16		★								★		★			★					
17		★								★		★						★		
18		★								★		★				★				
19		★										★			★					
20					★							★							★	★
					★				BONUS PAGES!					★		★		★		★
1			★		★			★	★	★										
2					★							★			★					
3					★			★		★						★				
4					★		★			★		★								
5								★		★					★					
6					★					★		★								★
7					★				★	★										
8			★										★		★					
9				★	★	★				★										
10			★		★					★					★					
11		★													★				★	

Skills Matrix

Day	Addition & Subtraction	Algebra & Ratios	Capitalization & Punctuation	Character Development	Data Analysis & Probability	Decimals & Percentages	Fitness	Fractions	Geometry & Measurement	Language Arts	Multiplication & Division	Parts of Speech	Problem Solving	Puzzles	Reading Comprehension	Science	Sentence Types & Structure	Social Studies	Usage	Writing
12					⭐					⭐		⭐								⭐
13		⭐					⭐	⭐		⭐							⭐			
14					⭐							⭐			⭐					
15		⭐								⭐					⭐	⭐				
16									⭐	⭐					⭐			⭐		
17					⭐										⭐					
18		⭐								⭐		⭐					⭐			
19										⭐			⭐						⭐	⭐
20		⭐													⭐		⭐			
BONUS PAGES!									⭐			⭐				⭐		⭐		⭐
1		⭐						⭐		⭐							⭐			⭐
2					⭐	⭐											⭐			⭐
3		⭐	⭐												⭐					
4	⭐	⭐					⭐			⭐			⭐							
5	⭐							⭐		⭐						⭐				
6	⭐	⭐											⭐		⭐					
7	⭐	⭐								⭐										
8	⭐	⭐											⭐		⭐					⭐
9	⭐									⭐					⭐					
10			⭐						⭐	⭐						⭐				
11									⭐	⭐						⭐				
12									⭐	⭐					⭐					
13			⭐	⭐					⭐	⭐										
14			⭐							⭐				⭐						⭐
15		⭐	⭐												⭐					
16		⭐								⭐						⭐	⭐			
17			⭐				⭐		⭐	⭐										
18									⭐							⭐	⭐			
19			⭐							⭐			⭐							⭐
20										⭐			⭐					⭐		
BONUS PAGES!																⭐		⭐		⭐

Summer Reading for Everyone

Reading is the single most important skill for school success. Experts recommend that sixth and seventh grade students read for at least 30 minutes each day. Help your child choose several books from this list based on his or her interests. Choose at least one fiction (F) and one nonfiction (NF) title. Then, head to the local library to begin your reading adventure!

If you like graphic novels...
Fish Girl
   by David Wiesner and Donna Jo Napoli (F)
All Summer Long
   by Hope Larson (F)

If you like funny books...
The Strange Case of Origami Yoda
   by Tom Angleberger (F)
Two Truths and a Lie
   by Ammi-Joan Paquette and Laurie Ann Thompson (NF)

If you like fantasy...
The Hobbit
   by J. R. R. Tolkien (F)
The Blue Sword
   by Robin McKinley (F)

If you like stories about history...
Fever 1793
   by Laurie Halse Anderson (F)
Code Name Pauline: Memoirs of a World War II Special Agent
   by Pearl Witherington Cornioley (NF)

If you like mysteries...
Chasing Vermeer
   by Blue Balliet (F)
Spirit Hunters
   by Ellen Oh (F)

If you like space...
The War of the Worlds
by H.G. Wells (F)
The Stars
by H.A. Rey (NF)

If you like science...
The Way Things Work
by David Macaulay (NF)
Generating Wind Power
by Niki Walker (NF)

If you like biographies...
Isaac the Alchemist
by Mary Losure (NF)
I Will Always Write Back: How One Letter Changed Two Lives
by Martin Ganda, Caitlin Alifirenka, and Liz Welch (NF)

If you like sports...
Rebound
by Kwame Alexander (F)
Rising Above
by Gregory, Elijah,
and Gabriel Zuckerman (NF)

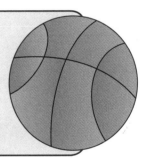

If you like nature...
Hatchet
by Gary Paulsen (F)
No Summit Out of Sight: The True Story of the Youngest Person to Climb the Seven Summits
by Jordan Romero and Linda LeBlanc (NF)

Summer Learning Is Everywhere!

Find learning opportunities wherever you go, all summer long!

Reading

- Make a book club with friends. Agree to read the same book and then talk about it while having snacks and a cold drink.

- Find two or three reviews for the same movie, book, or TV show. Read all of them and compare the reviewers' thoughts.

Language Arts

- Summarize a book, article, or movie for a friend and describe the main plot and characters to them.

- Practice writing in a journal. Experiment with different writing styles to find which you like more.

Math

- Research sudoku puzzles and make one of your own. Give it to a friend or family member and see how long it takes them to solve it.

- Measure the perimeter of a building where you spend a lot of time. Calculate the area from these measurements.

Science & Social Studies

- Ask 10 friends and family members where they were born. Mark all of these locations on a map, including where you were born. Determine who was born the farthest distance from where they live now.

- Pick one natural phenomenon that you have observed during the summer. Come up with an explanation for the phenomenon and do research to find out if you were right.

Character & Fitness

- Pay attention to the positive character traits in the people around you and make a list of the three most important ones to you.

- Learn how to use a new physical skill. It could be learning a new game, trying a new form of exercise, or building something. Keep trying until you feel confident.

Monthly Goals

A goal is something that you want to accomplish and must work toward. Sometimes, reaching a goal can be difficult.

Think of three goals to set for yourself this month. For example, you may want to exercise for 30 minutes each day. Write your goals on the lines. Post them someplace visible, where you will see them every day.

Place a check mark next to each goal that you complete. Feel proud that you have met your goals and set new ones to continue to challenge yourself.

1. _____

2. _____

3. _____

Word List

The following words are used in this section. Use a dictionary to look up each word that you do not know. Then, write three sentences. Use at least one word from the word list in each sentence.

conservation	polyps
cuneiform	radiocarbon dating
erosion	schedule
gridiron	sediment
organisms	tempo

1. _____

_____

2. _____

_____

3. _____

_____

Introduction to Flexibility

This section includes fitness and character development activities that focus on flexibility. These activities are designed to get you moving and thinking about building your physical fitness and your character. If you have limited mobility, feel free to modify any suggested exercises to fit your individual abilities.

Physical Flexibility

To the average person, *flexibility* means being able to accomplish everyday physical tasks easily, like bending to tie a shoe. These everyday tasks can be difficult for people whose muscles and joints have not been used and stretched regularly.

Proper stretching allows muscles and joints to move through their full range of motion, which is important for good flexibility. There are many ways that you stretch every day without realizing it. When you reach for a dropped pencil or a box of cereal on the top shelf, you are stretching your muscles. Flexibility is important to your health and growth, so challenge yourself to improve your flexibility consciously. Simple stretches and activities, such as yoga and tai chi, can improve your flexibility. Set a stretching goal for the summer, such as practicing daily until you can touch your toes.

Flexibility of Character

While it is important to have a flexible body, it is also important to be mentally flexible. Being mentally flexible means being open-minded to change. It can be disappointing when things do not go your way, but this is a normal reaction. Think of a time recently when unexpected circumstances ruined your plans. Maybe your mother had to work one weekend, and you could not go to a baseball game with friends because you needed to babysit a younger sibling. How did you deal with this situation?

A large part of being mentally flexible is realizing that there will be situations in life where unforeseen things happen. Often, it is how you react to the circumstances that affects the outcome. Arm yourself with tools to be flexible, such as having realistic expectations, brainstorming solutions to make a disappointing situation better, and looking for good things that may result from the initial disappointment.

Mental flexibility can take many forms. For example, being fair, respecting the differences of other people, and being compassionate are ways that you can practice mental flexibility. In difficult situations, remind yourself to be flexible, and you will reap the benefits of this important character trait.

Solve each problem.

1.
$$3,281$$
$$+1,952$$
$$5,233$$

2.
$$23.25$$
$$+\ 9.75$$
$$33.00$$

3.
$$62,523$$
$$-13,145$$
$$49,378$$

4.
$$66.70$$
$$-\ 1.954$$
$$64.746$$

5.
$$483$$
$$\times 367$$
$$3,381$$
$$28,980$$
$$144,900$$
$$177,261$$

6.
$$3.135$$
$$\times\ 789$$
$$28215$$
$$250800$$
$$2194500$$
$$2473.515$$

7.
$$0.92$$
$$\times\ 1.5$$
$$460$$
$$920$$
$$1.380$$

8.
$$4.18$$
$$\times\ 37$$
$$2926$$
$$12540$$
$$154.66$$

9. $6\overline{)9,468}$

10. $7\overline{)2,307}$

11. $8\overline{)10.4}$

12. $4\overline{)2.6}$

Look up each word in an online or print dictionary. Circle the syllable that is stressed. Then, write the word's definition on the line.

13. ignoble __not honorable in character or purpose__

14. specious _____

15. ersatz __made or used as a substitute__

16. debacle __a sudden failure a fiasco__

17. collateral _____

18. demean __cause a severe loss in the dignity of and respect__

DAY 1

Use the prefixes and suffixes and their meanings to write a definition for each word below.

Prefixes	Suffixes
re—back or again	ment—the act, result, or product of
dis—away, apart, or the opposite of	less—without or not
un—opposite, not, or lack of	
pre—before	

19. punishment _____

20. disappear _____

21. presoak _____

22. rewind _____

23. colorless_____

24. unsure _____

The scientific method is the process that scientists use when conducting experiments. Write the number of each step in the scientific method next to its description.

Step 1: Ask a Question   Step 2: Research the Topic

Step 3: Construct a Hypothesis   Step 4: Test and Observe

Step 5: Analyze and Draw Conclusions   Step 6: Report the Results

_____ A scientist studies the results and compares them to the original hypothesis.

_____ A scientist conducts the experiment, observes the results, and takes notes.

_____ A scientist asks *who*, *what*, *when*, *where*, and *why* about the topic.

_____ A scientist makes an informed prediction about the experiment's results.

_____ A scientist learns as much as possible about the topic.

_____ A scientist shares her hypothesis, method, and results with other scientists.

FACTOID: Antarctic ice is more than 2.6 miles (4.2 km) thick in some places.

Use exponents to rewrite each expression. Then, evaluate each expression.

EXAMPLE: $4 \times 4 \times 4 = 4^3 = 64$

1. $3 \times 3 \times 3 \times 3 \times 3 = $ _____ = _____
2. $7 \times 7 = $ _____ = _____
3. $4 \times 4 \times 4 \times 4 = $ _____ = _____
4. $2 \times 2 \times 2 \times 2 \times 2 \times 2 = $ _____ = _____
5. $9 \times 9 \times 9 = $ _____ = _____
6. $10 \times 10 \times 10 \times 10 \times 10 \times 10 \times 10 \times 10 = $ _____ = _____
7. $5 \times 5 \times 5 \times 5 = $ _____ = _____
8. $8 \times 8 \times 8 \times 8 = $ _____ = _____
9. $6 \times 6 \times 6 = $ _____ = _____

$$10^5$$

$$2^6$$

$$8^3$$

Write *C* on the line if the group of words is a complete sentence. Write *F* if the group of words is a sentence fragment. Write *R* if the group of words is a run-on sentence.

10. _____ The jockey mounted his horse.
11. _____ Whether there is enough food or not.
12. _____ We go swimming in the lake every summer it is always a lot of fun.
13. _____ We enjoyed the music.
14. _____ Loaned her favorite shirt to Alice.

Rewrite each sentence fragment as a complete sentence.

15. From high atop the stadium.

_____

_____

16. Hidden under the basket.

_____

_____

DAY 2

Circle the letter in front of the correct meaning for each root word. Then, write two words that contain the root word.

17. **bio**   A. sea   B. far   C. life

_____   _____

18. **pend**   A. one   B. before   C. hang

_____   _____

19. **path**   A. feeling   B. fear   C. all

_____   _____

20. **chron**   A. time   B. fear   C. study of

_____   _____

21. **port**   A. carry   B. out   C. in

_____   _____

On the left is a list of things that people in a society need. On the right is a list of services that a government may provide to meet those needs. Match each government service with a need by writing the letter on the line.

22. _____ education   A. printing money

23. _____ communication   B. building roads

24. _____ safety   C. funding and staffing public schools

25. _____ protection   D. providing a military

26. _____ transportation   E. setting and enforcing speed limits

27. _____ health   F. delivering mail

28. _____ help for the needy   G. making laws to restrict pollution

29. _____ clean air and water   H. building low-income housing

30. _____ money to trade for goods   I. inspecting food and drugs

FITNESS FLASH: Touch your toes 10 times.

* See page ii.

Write two equivalent fractions for each fraction.

1. $\frac{2}{4}$ = ___ = ___ 2. $\frac{2}{12}$ = ___ = ___ 3. $\frac{8}{14}$ = ___ = ___ 4. $\frac{4}{18}$ = ___ = ___

5. $\frac{10}{24}$ = ___ = ___ 6. $\frac{4}{9}$ = ___ = ___ 7. $\frac{10}{20}$ = ___ = ___ 8. $\frac{18}{24}$ = ___ = ___

Complete each equivalent fraction.

9. $\frac{1}{11} = \frac{}{33}$ 10. $\frac{1}{4} = \frac{}{20}$ 11. $\frac{4}{16} = \frac{}{32}$ 12. $\frac{8}{9} = \frac{}{54}$

13. $\frac{3}{15} = \frac{}{45}$ 14. $\frac{2}{6} = \frac{}{36}$ 15. $\frac{5}{16} = \frac{}{48}$ 16. $\frac{3}{8} = \frac{}{24}$

Correct the paragraph. Look for errors in capitalization and punctuation.

Plate Tectonics

Earth's crust is broken into huge pieces called tectonic plates these plates include whole continents and sections of the ocean floor. Tectonic plates. Are shifting constantly. The uneven line where two plates meet is called a rift zone earthquakes often occur along rift zones. When part of a slowly moving plate. Sticks to an opposing plate at a point along the rift zone, pressure builds. The pressure rises behind the section until finally it gives way and moves The shock from this sudden shift is like a stone tossed into a pond It sends waves in all directions

DAY 3

Read the passage. Then, answer the questions.

Energy Conservation

Energy conservation means being careful about how much energy you use and trying to use less energy. You can conserve energy by driving cars with higher fuel efficiency, which means you can travel farther using less fuel. You can recycle or reuse materials, such as plastic, glass, paper, and metal, and you can buy products made from recycled materials. You can also conserve energy by using less at home. Wear heavier clothing instead of turning up the heat when the weather gets colder. Turn off the lights when you leave a room and unplug small appliances and machines, such as televisions and computers, when you will be away for a long period of time. Using less electricity, gas, and water means you will have lower utility bills, and you will help the environment.

17. What is the main idea of this passage?
    A. Some materials can be recycled instead of thrown away.
    B. Utility bills are sometimes higher in the summer.
    C. There are many ways to conserve energy.

18. What does the phrase *energy conservation* mean?_____
    _____
    _____

19. Why might you want to use a car with high fuel efficiency?_____
    _____

20. What are some materials that can be recycled? _____
    _____
    _____

21. What are two ways that you can help conserve energy at home? _____
    _____
    _____
    _____

FACTOID: Global temperatures have risen 1.4°F (0.8°C) since 1880.

Find the greatest common factor (GCF) for each pair of numbers.

1.   6
       18
   GCF:

2.   15
      20
   GCF:

3.   24
      32
   GCF:

4.   14
      21
   GCF:

5.   14
      35
   GCF:

6.   9
      15
   GCF:

7.   18
      27
   GCF:

8.   4
      12
   GCF:

9.   15
      40
   GCF:

Read each sentence and decide what type of figurative language it contains. On the line, write S for simile, M for metaphor, H for hyperbole, or P for personification.

10. _____ Silence hung in the air like a thick veil of fog.

11. _____ I'm so hungry, I could eat a horse!

12. _____ Ian's tiny hands were like miniature starfish on his mama's arm.

13. _____ The drops of rain ran cheerfully down the window.

14. _____ The school was a complete zoo on the last day of class.

15. _____ This headache has been a bear all morning.

16. _____ The welcoming arms of Rodney's sleeping bag reached out to him as he sleepily crawled inside.

17. _____ My computer has been cranky and uncooperative all morning, so I haven't accomplished much.

18. _____ Hail bounced against the roof like thousands of tiny footsteps.

19. _____ Grandpa Harry worked his fingers to the bone for many years.

DAY 4

Circle the letter in front of the correct meaning for each root word. Then, write two words that contain the root word.

20. **therm**   A.   above   B.   heat   C.   after

    _____   _____

21. **aud**   A.   sound   B.   for   C.   taste

    _____   _____

22. **morph**   A.   love   B.   form   C.   change

    _____   _____

23. **biblio**   A.   form   B.   good   C.   book

    _____   _____

24. **geo**   A.   earth   B.   measure   C.   power

    _____   _____

Imagine that you are in charge of making a new television show that combines all of the characters from your two favorite shows. What would happen in the first episode of your new show? Use another sheet of paper if you need more space.

_____

_____

_____

_____

_____

_____

_____

_____

_____

FITNESS FLASH: Do 10 shoulder shrugs.

* See page ii.

DAY 5

Max is making some trail mix. The ratio of nuts to pieces of dried fruit is 3:1. Complete the ratio table to show equivalent ratios. Then, graph the ratios on the coordinate plane.

Nuts (x)	Fruit (y)
3	1
6	2
____	____
____	____
____	____

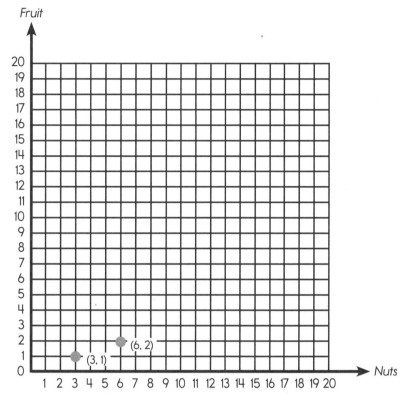

Write commas where they are needed in each sentence.

1. Gretchen can you give me a hand?

2. The mural was filled with splashes of blue green gold and red.

3. Mrs. Yim my fourth-grade teacher was always my favorite.

4. You can either come to my house or I will come to yours.

5. Carla donated food blankets and clothing.

6. "Please show me the way out of here" said Mia.

7. I want to leave but I am afraid that I will miss something.

8. On Saturday April 18 2009 I went swimming in Crystal Creek.

DAY 5

A *root word* is a word that has a prefix, a suffix, or both attached to it. Read each word. Write the root word and the prefix or suffix in the correct boxes.

	Prefix	Root Word	Suffix
9. misfortune			
10. remove			
11. painless			
12. unusual			
13. disappear			

Calf Stretch

Stretching is an important part of any exercise program. Stretching increases a person's range of motion and can prevent muscle injury. Remember to warm up before stretching by walking around the block or jogging in place for several minutes.

One important stretch for many athletes is the calf stretch. Your calf muscle extends from your heel to the back of your knee. Stand facing a wall. Raise both arms in front of you with the palms of your hands flat against the wall. Press against the wall. Position your right leg behind you, heel flat on the ground. Your left leg should be bent and slightly in front of your right leg, closer to the wall. You should feel the stretch along the lower back of your right leg. Hold the stretch for 30 seconds. Switch sides.

> **CHARACTER CHECK:** Think of someone you know who is courageous. Write a haiku poem about that person and share it with a family member.

* See page ii.

Find the least common multiple (LCM) for each set of numbers.

1.   6
     2
     LCM:

2.   4
     8
     LCM:

3.   5
     3
     LCM:

4.   4
     6
     LCM:

5.   8
     12
     LCM:

6.   6
     10
     LCM:

7.   6
     5
     15
     LCM:

8.   4
     9
     18
     LCM:

9.   4
     7
     14
     LCM:

Read each sentence. Circle the complete subject. Underline the complete predicate.

10. The robin is considered a sign of spring in the Midwest.

11. The Henderson family moved into an apartment on the 14th floor.

12. I read about the extra traffic that creates problems during the winter.

13. The US Open is a prestigious tennis tournament.

14. Each member of the team deserves a trophy for his participation and hard work.

15. Some rivers flow in a northern direction.

16. Chang's family went hiking in Yellowstone National Park.

17. Kelsey adopted the tiny gray kitten from the animal shelter.

18. Nora, Quinn, and Scott are going to the pool this afternoon.

DAY 6

Read the passage. Then, answer the questions.

Mountaintop Rescue

Sam Santiago groggily pulled himself out of sleep at the insistent ringing of his cell phone. Moments later, he hurriedly dressed in the dim glow from the hallway night-light. When his wife woke up, she sighed. "Who is it this time?" she asked.

"A dozen Boy Scouts and their chaperones," replied Sam, slipping on a second pair of socks. "Over two feet of snow fell on the mountain last night, and the Scouts and their leaders were unprepared. No one's heard anything from them, and the parents are understandably frantic."

"I'm heading for the airport," he added, grabbing his keys from the dresser.

"Oh, those poor boys," said Isobel, reaching for her glasses. She was fully awake now.

"Do you really think it's safe to fly, Sam?" she asked, anxiously peering out the window at the steadily falling flakes. "Your visibility is going to be nearly nonexistent with this snow."

"I wouldn't go if didn't think I had the ability to bring them home safely," Sam promised. "You know that, Isobel. I won't take any unnecessary risks."

In spite of his reassurances to Isobel, Sam felt a wave of worry wash over him as he stood next to the helicopter. He took a deep breath of the icy air and prepared himself for a long night.

19. Write a brief summary of the passage._____
    _____

20. Does Sam reveal his feelings about the rescue to Isobel? Why or why not?
    _____

21. What metaphor does the author use in the last paragraph? _____
    _____

22. How do you think Isobel feels about Sam's job? Cite examples from the text to
    support your answer. _____
    _____

23. What do you think happens next in the story? On a separate sheet of paper, continue and conclude the story.

Rewrite each pair of fractions using the least common denominator (LCD).

1. $\frac{1}{9}$ and $\frac{1}{3}$

2. $\frac{1}{3}$ and $\frac{1}{6}$

3. $\frac{5}{6}$ and $\frac{2}{5}$

4. $\frac{3}{8}$ and $\frac{2}{3}$

5. $\frac{1}{3}$ and $\frac{4}{9}$

6. $\frac{4}{5}$ and $\frac{5}{9}$

7. $\frac{2}{4}$ and $\frac{3}{7}$

8. $\frac{2}{3}$ and $\frac{7}{8}$

9. $\frac{3}{5}$ and $\frac{5}{6}$

Underline the subject in each sentence. Then, circle the correct form of the verb.

10. Some of the beads (is, are) missing from the necklace.

11. Where (is, are) the gate to her house?

12. Tucson (lies, lie) to the south of Phoenix, Arizona.

13. A statue of Barbara Johns (stand, stands) on capital grounds in Virginia.

14. The Dodgers, Braves, and Cardinals (is, are) division leaders.

Complete each sentence with a verb that makes sense and agrees with the subject.

15. Brittany and Mel _____ their homework immediately after school.

16. If the sheep are in the meadow, the cows _____ in the barn.

17. Tourists _____ warmer climates in the winter.

18. Christie _____ much more slowly than Merilee.

19. The home team fans always_____ louder than the visiting team fans.

DAY 7

Read each word. Write the root word and the prefix or suffix in the correct boxes. Some words may have both a prefix and a suffix.

	Prefix	Root Word	Suffix
20. misspelled			
21. disagree			
22. reappearing			
23. hopeless			
24. unlikely			

The puzzles below use letters and words as clues to represent an idea, a phrase, or a saying. The placement and size of the words may help convey a puzzle's meaning. Look at the puzzles. Write the phrase, saying, or idea that each clue represents.

25.

Funny   Funny

Words   Words

Words   Words

_____

26.

All world

_____

27.

thodeepught

_____

28.

PRO

MISE

_____

FITNESS FLASH: Touch your toes 10 times.

* See page ii.

16

Graph the following points on the coordinate plane: *A* (4, 6), *B* (4, –3), *C* (–2, –3).

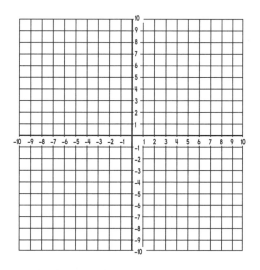

Points *A*, *B*, and *C* form three vertices of a rectangle. The fourth vertex is point *D*. Connect the points on the grid to determine the location of point *D*. Write its coordinates: *D* (_____, _____).

Complete each proverb with a word from the word bank. Then, explain what the proverb means.

| actions | fonder | hand | greener | cloud |

1. A bird in _____ is worth two in the bush.

   _____

2. Absence makes the heart grow _____.

   _____

3. Every _____ has a silver lining.

   _____

4. The grass is always _____ on the other side of the fence.

   _____

5. _____ speak louder than words.

   _____

DAY 8

Many foreign words and phrases are commonly used in English. Read each sentence. Write the meaning of the italicized word or phrase on the line. Use a dictionary if you need help.

6. At the party, Ren spilled fruit punch on the carpet and was embarrassed by his *faux pas.*_____

7. Because there is little traffic there, Janice rides her bike around the *cul-de-sac* in her neighborhood. _____

8. In order to apply for a job as senior editor, Sam submitted his *résumé* to the human resources department. _____

9. My music teacher insists that my *forte* is rhythm. _____

Write the letter of each type of scientist next to the description of what the scientist studies. Use a dictionary if you need help.

A.	agronomists	B.	anthropologists	C	botanists
D.	ecologists	E.	entomologists	F.	geneticists
G.	marine biologists	H.	paleontologists	I.	zoologists

10. _____ plant life

11. _____ living and nonliving things in ecosystems

12. _____ relationships of organisms through DNA

13. _____ farms, crops, and soil

14. _____ animals and their classifications

15. _____ insects

16. _____ fossils and life forms of the past

17. _____ past and present-day human beings

18. _____ aquatic animals and plants

FACTOID: Every day, the human body replaces millions of worn-out cells.

Solve the problems. Show your work.

1. $12\overline{)1{,}584}$

2. $73\overline{)84{,}649}$

3. $25\overline{)4{,}675}$

4. $19\overline{)24{,}396}$

5. $45\overline{)5{,}947}$

6. $60\overline{)588{,}140}$

7. $105\overline{)212{,}205}$

8. $15\overline{)87{,}129}$

9. $54\overline{)749{,}423}$

Correct the paragraph. Look for errors in subject/verb agreement.

Monday Math Challenge

Every Monday, students in Mrs. Verdan's class works in pairs to complete math

challenges. Each pair select its own working space. Gregory and Lea likes the table by

the window. Lily and Masandra takes the round table near the door. Mandy and Zoe

grabs the soft seats in the library corner. Each pair has 45 minutes to solve the puzzle.

Most of them finishes on time. They shares their solutions with the whole class.

Mrs. Verdan explain the solution and answer questions. Mrs. Verdan's students enjoys the

weekly math challenges.

DAY 9

Read the passage. Then, answer the questions.

Hammurabi's Code

One reason that modern countries run smoothly is that their laws are published. Because of this, all citizens know the laws that they must follow. During ancient times, laws were not always recorded. A Babylonian king named Hammurabi created the first set of written laws for his people around 1760 BC. He wanted to bring all of the people in his empire together under one set of laws. Because the laws were written, everyone, whether rich or poor, was expected to obey them.

Hammurabi's Code included 282 laws written in cuneiform, a type of writing in which symbols were carved into clay tablets. Each law included a penalty, or punishment, for disobeying it. The laws were written on a **stela**, which was a large slab of stone posted for all to see. Archaeologists working in the area now known as Iran discovered the stela in 1901. Hammurabi's Code is now displayed in the Louvre Museum in Paris, France.

10. What is the main idea of this passage?
    A. Modern countries publish their laws.
    B. Hammurabi's Code is an ancient set of written laws.
    C. Archaeologists often find ancient materials.

11. Who was Hammurabi? _____
    _____

12. Why did Hammurabi write his laws? _____
    _____
    _____
    _____

13. What is a *stela*? _____
    _____

14. Visit a library or go online to find examples of cuneiform. How do the examples
    add to your understanding of the selection?_____
    _____

FITNESS FLASH: Do arm circles for 30 seconds.

* See page ii.

Use equal ratios to solve each problem.

1. The Quick-Mart grocery store sells 5 bottles of water for $2.00. How many bottles of water can a customer buy with $12.00?

   _____ bottles of water

2. The tomato plants in Ms. Lang's garden grow 2 inches every 3 days. How much will they grow in 15 days?

   _____ inches

3. Oscar drove 240 miles in 4 hours. How far will he drive in 7 hours?

   _____ miles

4. Roberto scored 3 points in 2 soccer games. At this rate, how many points will he score in 10 games?

   _____ points

This glossary is from a book about nutrition. Use it to answer the questions that follow.

calorie: a measure of the energy stored in food; the amount of heat needed to raise the temperature of one gram of water one degree Celsius

digestion: the process of breaking up food into smaller parts so that the body can use the nutrients in the food

nutrients: the building blocks, such as carbohydrates, proteins, fats, vitamins, and minerals, of various cell parts

protein: nutrients that build, maintain, and repair the tissues in the body; meat, nuts, seeds, dairy products, and legumes are good sources of protein

vitamins: nutrients that are essential in small quantities for normal health and are needed for chemical reactions in the cells

5. If the word *carbohydrates* were added to the glossary, where would it belong?

   _____

6. Which of these would not be a good source of protein?
   A. lettuce   B. chicken   C. black beans

7. Give an example of two types of nutrients. _____ _____

8. What is a calorie? _____

DAY 10

An *anagram* is a word that is made by rearranging the letters of another word. Write the anagrams that best fit each pair of clues.

9.   a type of cup _____

    candy that is chewed repeatedly _____

10.   item worn by babies _____

    got back money that was loaned _____

11.   a circle _____

    a place to swim that some people have in their yards _____

12.   the rising and falling of the ocean level _____

    to correct a piece of writing _____

13.   to move smoothly _____

    a hunting animal that lives in a pack _____

Respect means treating people with courtesy and consideration. Think about a time when you saw a person show respect. Where were you? How did the person demonstrate respect? Choose one of the following situations. On another sheet of paper, draw a four-panel comic strip showing possible outcomes of people being respectful and disrespectful.

A.   It is the last week of school before summer vacation. You and your best friends are talking after lunch and enjoying being outdoors. Then, you hear the bell ring. Everyone walks toward the school and arrives at the entrance at the same time.

B.   You are in the school cafeteria eating lunch with your friends. Students are busy eating and talking, and the room is very noisy. Suddenly, you notice that the principal has entered the cafeteria and is ready to make an announcement.

CHARACTER CHECK: Make a list of three things you can do at home that demonstrate cooperation. Post the list so that family members can add to it.

Order from least to greatest.

1. –5, 7, 3, –2, 0, –7

_____

2. 3, –3, 2, –2, 4, –5

_____

3. 10, –12, 11, –1, 0, 5

_____

4. –8, 12, 5, –3, 2, –2

_____

Find the absolute value of each integer.

5. |–24| = _____   6. |35| = _____

7. |56| = _____   8. |–82| = _____

9. |16| = _____   10. |–39| = _____

Write each ratio as a fraction in simplest form.

11. There are 5 horses and 15 elephants in a circus. Write the ratio of elephants to horses. _____

12. There are 16 horses and 14 elephants in a circus. Write the ratio of horses to elephants. _____

13. There are 11 blue marbles and 7 red marbles in a box. Write the ratio of red marbles to blue marbles. _____

14. There are 12 apples and 15 oranges in a fruit basket. Write the ratio of apples to oranges. _____

15. There are 5 blue marbles and 16 red marbles in a box. Write the ratio of blue marbles to red marbles. _____

16. There are 12 dogs and 7 cats in a park. Write the ratio of cats to dogs.

_____

DAY 11

Portmanteau words are made by combining two words. For example, *brunch* is a combination of the words *breakfast* and *lunch*. Combine each pair of words to make a portmanteau word.

17. flame + glare = _____

18. smoke + fog = _____

19. crispy + munch = _____

20. motor + hotel = _____

21. gleam + shimmer = _____

Label each map feature with a word from the word bank.

compass rose	legend	scale	title

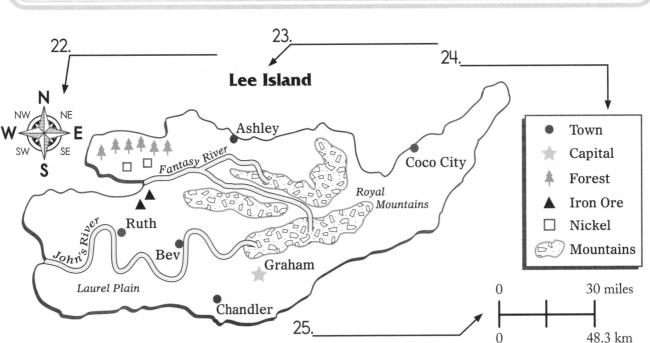

22. _____

23. _____

24. _____

Lee Island

N
NW   NE
W   E
SW   SE
S

Ashley

Fantasy River

Coco City

Royal
Mountains

Ruth

Bev

John's River

Graham

Laurel Plain

Chandler

25. _____

●	Town
★	Capital
♠	Forest
▲	Iron Ore
☐	Nickel
	Mountains

0   30 miles

0   48.3 km

FACTOID: The Peregrine falcon can fly at speeds up to 186 miles (300 km) per hour.

Solve each problem.

1.
$$7.59 \\ +2.09$$

2.
$$25.90 \\ +34.80$$

3.
$$157.8 \\ +\ 30.4$$

4.
$$83.041 \\ +\ 5.226$$

5.
$$10.42 \\ -\ 6.01$$

6.
$$52.99 \\ -25.00$$

7.
$$14.07 \\ -\ 2.88$$

8.
$$19.99 \\ -12.70$$

9.
$$15.08 \\ 46.09 \\ +145.73$$

10.
$$35.33 \\ 19.38 \\ +10.94$$

11.
$$19.44 \\ -11.79$$

12.
$$99.421 \\ -77.025$$

A *concrete noun* is a person, a place, or a thing. An *abstract noun* is an idea, an emotion, or a concept. Write *C* if the word is a concrete noun. Write *A* if the word is an abstract noun.

13. _____ joy

14. _____ bravery

15. _____ hair

16. _____ imagination

17. _____ peach

18. _____ freedom

19. _____ phone

20. _____ guitar

Is the noun *pride* a concrete noun or an abstract noun? Explain your decision.

_____

_____

_____

_____

_____

_____

DAY 12

Read each sentence. Then, circle the letter next to the correct meaning of the boldfaced word.

21. The engineers were afraid that the bridge would **buckle** under too much weight.
    A. piece of metal worn in the middle of a belt
    B. collapse or give way under pressure

22. The committee will **deliberate** on the issues.
    A. discuss before making a decision
    B. done on purpose after careful consideration

23. Please **relay** my message to the principal.
    A. communicate or pass along to
    B. race with a team of runners

24. We **scoured** the park for clues to the mystery.
    A. scrubbed clean
    B. searched thoroughly

25. A **plume** of smoke rose from the chimney.
    A. feather of a bird
    B. long column or band

If you could choose, would you rather be able to fly or to become invisible? Why? What other superpower would you like to have? Use another sheet of paper if you need more space.

_____

_____

_____

_____

_____

FITNESS FLASH: Practice a V-sit. Stretch five times.

* See page ii.

Use the ratios to convert each measurement.

1. 3 yards = _____ feet

2. _____ cups = 5 gallons

3. 72 inches = _____ yards

4. _____ ounces = 5 pounds

5. _____ inches = 7 feet

6. 24 feet = _____ yards

7. 40 pints = _____ gallons

8. 16 cups = _____ quarts

9. _____ inches = 4 yards

10. 48 ounces = _____ pounds

inches to feet = 12:1

feet to yards = 3:1

inches to yards = 36:1

ounces to pounds = 16:1

cups to quarts = 4:1

pints to gallons = 8:1

Writing is more interesting to read when it includes a variety of sentence structures. Write a sentence to fit each description.

11. Write a complex sentence.

_____

12. Write a sentence with an indirect object.

_____

13. Write a compound sentence that contains a prepositional phrase.

_____

14. Write a sentence with a compound subject and/or verb.

_____

15. Write a sentence with two direct objects.

_____

DAY 13

Read the movie schedule. Then, answer the questions.

Summer Movies
Afternoon and Evening Schedule

Cinema 6	Movie Mania	Theater Town
Oceans Apart 12:30 2:15 4:30	*Your Lucky Day* 12:30 2:15 4:30 7:00	*Feline Friends* 1:00 3:30 5:00
Land of Treasure 12:15 2:30 5:00	*Land of Treasure* 12:15 2:45 5:30 7:30	*Gridiron Greats* 1:00 3:15 5:30
Gridiron Greats 1:00 3:00 5:30	*Gridiron Greats* 1:30 4:00	*Time and Time Again* 12:30 3:45 6:15
Super Safari 1:00 3:30 6:00	*Super Safari* 2:30 5:30	*Your Lucky Day* 12:15 3:00 5:00
Your Lucky Day 12:00 3:30	*Oceans Apart* 3:00 6:00	*The Prairie Pals* 2:00 5:15
The Prairie Pals 12:00 3:30 6:15	*Feline Friends* 12:15 2:45 5:00	*Land of Treasure* 12:00 3:45 6:30

16. Which movie is scheduled for the latest show time at any of the theaters?

_____

17. It is 12:15 P.M. Valerie has a scout meeting at 4:00 P.M. Her family would like to see a movie before the meeting. Which of the following movies would fit their schedule, if each movie is two hours long?

    A. *Oceans Apart* at Movie Mania   B. *Gridiron Greats* at Theater Town

    C. *Your Lucky Day* at Cinema 6   D. *Super Safari* at Movie Mania

18. There are three children in the Sanchez family. Each child wants to see a different movie. Which of the theaters is showing three different movies with the same starting time?

_____

FACTOID: Africa's Sahara Desert is the size of the United States.

Solve each problem. Show your work.

Mrs. Carlyle bought a bag of peanuts for her children. When Phillip, Joy, Brent, and Preston came home from school, they each took some peanuts from the bag.

- Phillip took $\frac{1}{3}$ of the peanuts from the bag.

- Joy took $\frac{1}{4}$ of the remaining peanuts.

- Brent took $\frac{1}{2}$ of the remaining peanuts.

- Preston took 10 peanuts.

- There were 71 peanuts remaining in the bag.

1. How many peanuts were originally in the bag? _____

2. How many peanuts did each child take? _____

_____

Rewrite each sentence to correct the double negative.

3. Sidney couldn't do nothing with her hair.

_____

4. Mateo didn't have no second thoughts about the decision he made.

_____

5. No, Celia didn't see nobody else at the market.

_____

6. Kevin could not never see the road because of the heavy snow.

_____

7. Mia hasn't received no mail in more than a week.

_____

8. I didn't borrow none of the movies from Toni.

_____

DAY 14

Read each sentence. Then, circle the letter next to the correct meaning of the boldfaced word.

9. Deanna's **rash** decision caused her to lose the game.
    A.   hasty or reckless
    B.   skin inflammation

10. Mom paid a **toll** when we crossed the bridge.
    A.   ring like a bell
    B.   small tax or fee

11. Her **initial** reaction to the rain was to cancel the race.
    A.   first or beginning
    B.   the first letter of a person's name

12. The river has a very high **bank**.
    A.   a place to keep money
    B.   a slope or hill

13. We asked the cashier to **void** our transaction.
    A.   cancel
    B.   empty space

How would your life change without electricity and machines like cars? Describe the things in your life that would change and the things that would stay the same. Would life be better or worse? Why? Use another sheet of paper if you need more space.

_____

_____

_____

_____

_____

FITNESS FLASH: Do arm circles for 30 seconds.

* See page ii.

Translate each description into an algebraic expression. Then, evaluate the expression using the value shown in the box for the variable.

EXAMPLE: the quotient of 112 and *a* added to 25 = (112 ÷ *a*) + 25 = 53

a = 4	*b* = 3	*c* = 9	*d* = 2
w = 10	*x* = 11	*y* = 7	*z* = 5

1. the difference of 100 and the product of *y* and 12 = _____ = ____

2. *b* times the sum of 15 and 37 = _____ = ____

3. 27 added to the product of *z* and 12 = _____ = ____

4. 135 divided by the product of *c* and 5 = _____ = ____

5. *w* to the second power times the quotient of 12 and 4 = _____ = ____

6. 12 times *d* divided by the difference of 25 and 19 = _____ = ____

7. the product of *x* and 5 added to 13 = _____ = ____

An *antecedent* is the word or phrase to which a pronoun refers. Underline the antecedent in each sentence. Then, circle the pronoun that agrees in number with the antecedent.

8. Our neighbor brought (her, their) dog to play at our house.

9. Since it has been getting cold, I told the guests to bring (his, their, your) coats.

10. The lawyer often collaborates with (our, her, their) colleagues.

11. Students who complete all of (his, her, their) homework assignments often do well on tests.

12. If anyone else wants to go on the field trip, (he or she, it, they) should bring a note from home tomorrow.

13. The girl needs to have (her, she, their) own art supplies for class.

14. The council members voiced (his, her, their) opinions at the town hall meeting.

DAY 15

Read each sentence. Then, circle the letter next to the correct meaning of the boldfaced word.

15. To what **degree** do you agree with his remarks?
    A. measurement of temperature
    B. extent of a condition

16. The tapestry has **elaborate** designs on it.
    A. detailed or complex
    B. tell more about

17. The map has a **legend** to tell us what the symbols mean.
    A. story told from the past
    B. explanation of symbols

18. The bike shop charges a **flat** rate for replacing tires.
    A. set or not varying
    B. smooth and even

19. Mom said that my new glasses **suit** me.
    A. look appropriate on
    B. matched set of clothing

Dance Fever!

Show off your ability to dance to different musical tempos. Choose songs that have different speeds and have a friend or adult play small parts of each song. Start dancing and adjust your speed to each song's tempo. Stretch all of your major muscle groups with movements such as bending forward, arching your back, and lifting your arms above your head. Remember to warm up and cool down with a slow song and stretch slowly at first.

CHARACTER CHECK: Make a list of three things you can do at home to show respect. Share your list with a family member.

Write equivalent expressions.

1. $5(a + a + a) =$ _____

2. $6(3x - 4) =$ _____

3. $3^2(g + 12) =$ _____

4. $w(3w - 8) =$ _____

5. $10(5 + 2m) =$ _____

6. $13(z + z + z) =$ _____

7. $3(3y + 7) =$ _____

8. $5(b + 20) =$ _____

9. $4^2(2c + 3) =$ _____

10. $9(9d - d) =$ _____

11. $7(n^2 + 8) =$ _____

12. $40 \div 6(f + f + f) =$ _____

Circle the pronoun or pronouns that correctly complete each sentence.

13. (I, Me) planted many seeds in (our, ours) garden.

14. Will (you, your) come with (I, me) to (their, theirs) house?

15. Joe loaned (he, his) new baseball glove to (she, her).

16. Did (her, she) blame (we, us) for the broken window?

17. Tye will help Justin and (I, me) look for (it, its).

18. (We, Us) can build (it, its) over there in (your, yours) big tree.

19. Owen and (I, me) took an art course this summer.

20. Sara and Bonnie took (they, them) to the matinee.

21. After the snowstorm, (us, we) helped shovel the walkway.

22. Cameron helped (she, her) find the lens from (her, hers) glasses.

DAY 16

Read the passage. Then, answer the questions.

Fossils

Fossils are the remains of plants or animals from thousands of years ago that have turned to stone. After the organisms died, their bodies were buried in sediment and gradually replaced by minerals. Sometimes, an animal's bones, teeth, or shell are preserved. Other times, only an impression of its body is made. Footprints, eggs, and nests can also be fossilized.

Fossils can be found in many places. They are frequently uncovered when people dig up the earth as they build roads. Also, fossils often are buried in layers of rock and are exposed through erosion of a mountainside. Others are found during undersea excavation. Scientists study fossils to learn what the living animals and plants looked like. They can use radiocarbon dating to find out how old a fossil is. All living things contain carbon, so scientists measure how much carbon is left in a fossil to determine its age.

23. What is the main idea of this passage?
    A. Radiocarbon dating helps scientists determine the age of fossils.
    B. Sometimes, only an impression of a plant is left.
    C. Fossils are plant or animal remains from long ago.

24. What happens when something is fossilized?_____
    _____

25. What parts of an animal's body might be preserved? _____
    _____

26. Why do scientists study fossils?_____
    _____

27. How does radiocarbon dating help determine a fossil's age?_____
    _____
    _____
    _____

FACTOID: There are approximately twice as many kangaroos in Australia as there are people.

A *dependent variable* is a value that is affected by other values in a problem or situation. An *independent variable* is a value that affects the outcome of the dependent variable.

In each situation, identify the dependent variable and the independent variable. Then, write an equation to solve the problem.

1. Maria has to buy oranges at the grocery store. Oranges cost $1.15 per pound. How much will Maria spend on oranges?

    Dependent variable: _____

    Independent variable: _____

    Equation: _____

2. When a lilac bush is planted, it is 24 inches tall. Each month, it grows 6 inches taller. How tall will it get over time?

    Dependent variable: _____

    Independent variable: _____

    Equation: _____

Circle each possessive pronoun. Draw an arrow to the noun that it modifies.

3. Their mom travels around the state on business.

4. Our house is near the library.

5. Its handle is loose.

6. The black dog beside the tree is mine.

7. Her socks are in the middle drawer.

8. We went to the musical with his parents.

9. The house with the pool is his.

10. My friend asked my opinion about which bike to buy.

11. The vegetable and cream cheese sandwich is hers.

12. Their wooded backyard is a great place to play.

DAY 17

The emotion associated with a word is its connotation. Read each word. Write *P* if the word has a positive connotation. Write *N* if the word has a negative connotation. Then, find each word in a dictionary and write its denotation.

13. _____ desolate _____

14. _____ serene _____

15. _____ noble _____

16. _____ betray _____

17. _____ intrepid _____

Unscramble each word to form the name of an Eastern or Western European country. Use a map if you need help.

18. diarnel _____

19. saursi _____

20. ngeyram _____

21. atruisa _____

22. kndaemr _____

23. ktuery _____

24. dsewne _____

25. tlaiva _____

26. apgrotlu _____

27. rsuelba _____

FITNESS FLASH: Practice a V-sit. Stretch five times.

* See page ii.

Use substitution to determine which value for the variable makes the equation or inequality true. Then, circle the value that makes the number sentence true.

1. $x + 25 = 51$ 24, 25, 26
2. $17 \times a = 85$ 9, 7, 5
3. $26 > 7 \times y$ 5, 4, 3
4. $35 < 57 - d$ 20, 25, 30
5. $6m > 72$ 13, 12, 11
6. $p - 84 > 102$ 184, 186, 188
7. $125 \div t = 25$ 4, 5, 6
8. $n + 55 > 175$ 125, 120, 115

Circle the indefinite pronouns in each sentence.

9. Many will come to the museum this summer.

10. A hummingbird came to the feeder this morning, and others came last night.

11. Someone got the crowd to cheer excitedly.

12. Only a few registered, but several arrived on the day of the race.

13. I think somebody should clean up the marbles and game pieces.

14. Walter and Mason are here with a mower; either can mow the yard.

15. Anybody who gets home before me can put dinner in the oven.

16. Fruits and vegetables are delicious; each is good for a healthy, growing body.

17. Jessie liked the sweaters and wanted to buy both.

18. Some have blue tags, and others have red tags.

FITNESS FLASH: Do 10 shoulder shrugs.

DAY 18

Read each pair of words. Write *P* next to the word with a positive connotation. Write *N* next to the word with a negative connotation. Then, look up each word in a dictionary and write its denotation.

19. _____ thrifty _____

_____ cheap _____

20. _____ picky _____

_____ selective _____

21. _____ pushy _____

_____ assertive _____

22. _____ haughty _____

_____ proud _____

How are animal cells and plant cells alike? How are they different? For each cell characteristic below, write *plant*, *animal*, or *both* on the line.

23. _____ These cells have cell membranes.

24. _____ These cells use chloroplasts for photosynthesis.

25. _____ These cells use mitosis to divide into two daughter cells.

26. _____ Each of these cells has one or more large vacuoles.

27. _____ Instead of a few large vacuoles, these cells have several small vacuoles.

28. _____ These cells have cell walls that usually give the cells a rectangular shape.

29. _____ Each of these cells has a nucleus that controls all of the cell's functions.

30. _____ These cells have irregular shapes.

31. _____ Mitochondria help create energy for these cells.

FACTOID: An adult elephant can eat 550 pounds (249.5 kg) of vegetation each day.

Solve each equation to find the value of the variable.

1. $y + 8 = 11$

2. $x + 8 = 24$

3. $v + 3 = 13$

4. $m - 12 = 5$

5. $q - 15 = 100$

6. $r - 19 = 37$

7. $w \times 4 = 32$

8. $z \div 12 = 3$

9. $a \div 6 = 7$

10. $11 \times y = 88$

11. $g \div 5 = 12$

12. $c \times 15 = 75$

A *reflexive pronoun* indicates that a person or thing is both initiating and receiving the action of a sentence. Underline the reflexive pronoun in each sentence.

13. The woman in Leonardo da Vinci's famous painting, the *Mona Lisa*, seems to be smiling to herself.

14. For centuries, people have asked themselves why this is so.

15. I have wondered myself about her mysterious smile.

16. Leonardo da Vinci kept that secret to himself.

17. If you want to see the *Mona Lisa* for yourself, go to the Louvre Museum in Paris, France.

Complete each sentence with the correct reflexive pronoun in parentheses.

18. Leonardo developed a new painting technique by _____. (itself, himself)

19. The wall _____ was Leonardo's canvas. (himself, itself)

20. I have tried the technique _____ and found it challenging. (myself, ourselves)

DAY 19

Read the passage. Then, answer the questions.

The Great Barrier Reef

The Great Barrier Reef is considered by many people to be one of the seven natural wonders of the world. The reef stretches for more than 1,200 miles (1,931 km) off the coast of northeast Australia. It is the largest coral structure in the world, the largest structure ever constructed by living organisms, and the only living thing on Earth that is visible from outer space.

The Great Barrier Reef consists mostly of coral, a rocklike substance made by tiny animals. These tiny animals, called *polyps*, are too numerous to count. The polyps are born in a continuous cycle of reproducing, eating, and dying. New coral is slowly added to the reef through this process.

The fragile reef is continually changing its shape and color. These changes are caused by many factors, including the polyps' constant activities. People visiting the reef and changes in the environment can damage the reef through pollution or carelessness. Harmful animals, such as the crown of thorns starfish, can also destroy the reef, especially when environmental changes contribute to their **overpopulation**.

21.   The tiny animals that make the Great Barrier Reef are called _____ .

22.   Where is the Great Barrier Reef located? _____

_____

23.   Circle the letter next to each statement that is true.
   A.   The Great Barrier Reef has not changed for centuries.
   B.   The Great Barrier Reef stretches for more than 1,200 miles (1,931 km).
   C.   The Great Barrier Reef can be seen from outer space.
   D.   The Great Barrier Reef is the second largest coral structure in the world.

24.   What does the word *overpopulation* mean?_____

25.   Write three factors that cause the reef to change._____

_____

_____

26.   How do you think the author feels abut the Great Barrier Reef? Explain.

_____

_____

Describe each set of data.

1. Scores on a math test: 77, 79, 85, 88, 88, 92, 94, 98, 99

   Lowest value: _____   Highest value: _____

   Spread: _____   Center value: _____

2. Visitors to a museum each hour during operating hours: 35, 42, 65, 59, 84, 62, 46, 52, 24

   Lowest value: _____   Highest value: _____

   Spread: _____   Center value: _____

3. Weight of cats, in pounds: 9, 11, 11, 12, 14, 14, 15, 15, 16, 17, 18, 18, 20, 22

   Lowest value: _____   Highest value: _____

   Spread: _____   Center value: _____

Draw a line through each incorrectly used pronoun. Write the correct pronoun above it.

Art Club Memo

Dear Craft Club Members,

Whomever forgot to return the scissors should bring it back to the art room. A few pairs were missing from the room after our meeting. In the future, someone will be allowed to remove supplies from the room. The school trusts us, and we have a responsibility to leave the workspace as we found them. I am sure that these was a mistake. That is why I am asking each member to check he backpack. Call me if you find they. Thank you for you help!

Sincerely,

Liz

DAY 20

Read each sentence. Draw a line through each modifier that needs to be removed. If a new modifier is needed, write it on the line.

4. We don't hardly have time to watch television. _____

5. Your answer doesn't make no difference to her. _____

6. My sisters work even more harder than I do. _____

7. Kobe does good in all of his subjects at school. _____

8. Benny is tallest than me. _____

9. There are so many choices that I don't know which one I like more. _____

10. I couldn't hardly believe that my parents let me get a dog. _____

11. This cake is gooder than the pie that you bought. _____

12. He is one of the most funniest people I know. _____

13. This painting is more prettier than that one. _____

When you go to a fair or an amusement park, do you prefer to ride the rides, play games, eat food, or watch people? Why is that activity your favorite? Use another sheet of paper if you need more space.

_____

_____

_____

_____

_____

_____

_____

CHARACTER CHECK: Throughout the day, look for people who are encouraging others. At the end of the day, talk with a family member about the encouragement you observed.

The Heart of the Matter

How does exercise affect your heart rate?

Each time the ventricles of your heart contract, blood is forced into your arteries. Each heartbeat makes your arteries stretch, which causes the pulsing sensation that you feel. As blood is being pushed out of your heart, it moves very quickly so that it can reach parts of your body that are far from your heart.

Materials:

- watch with a second hand

Procedure:

Sit on the floor or in a chair and relax for one minute. Use your index and middle fingers to locate your pulse in either your wrist or neck. Count the number of times that you feel your heart beat for 15 seconds. Multiply this number by four. This will be your resting pulse rate for one minute. Record this number on the chart below.

Jog in place for one minute. Then, stop jogging and use your index and middle fingers to locate your pulse in your wrist or neck. Count the number of times that you feel your heart beat for 15 seconds. Multiply this number by four. Record this number in the "Active Heart Rate" column. Repeat these steps two additional times. Then, calculate your average resting and active heart rates by adding the three trials and dividing by three. Finally, answer the question below.

Results:

Trial	Resting Heart Rate	Active Heart Rate
1		
2		
3		
Average:		

How did exercise affect your heart rate? _____

_____

* See page ii.

BONUS

Newton's First Law

Will an object at rest stay at rest and an object in motion stay in motion unless acted upon by another force? In this activity, you will test Newton's first law.

Materials:
- plastic cup
- coin
- index card

Procedure:
Cover the top of the cup with the index card. Put the coin on top of the card. Think about how you can get the coin inside of the cup without touching the coin or lifting or tilting the index card.

Test your ideas and see if you can get the coin into the cup. After you have gotten the coin into the cup, answer each question.

1. How did you get the coin into the cup? _____

    _____

    _____

2. What happens to the coin if the card is moved away slowly?

    _____

    _____

3. Why does the coin drop into the cup? _____

    _____

    _____

    _____

4. Can you think of a place where you have seen something similar happen?

    _____

    _____

    _____

Latitude and Longitude

Write the name of the North American city that is found at each latitude and longitude reading.

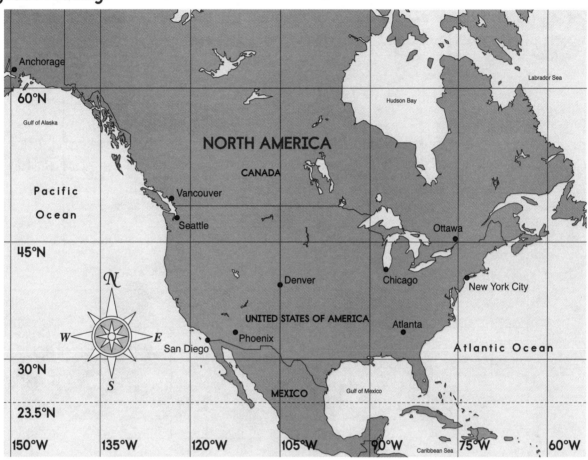

1. 61°13'N, 149°54'W

    _____

2. 33°45'N, 84°23'W

    _____

3. 41°50'N, 87°37'W

    _____

4. 39°45'N, 105°W

    _____

5. 47°37'N, 122°20'W

    _____

6. 33°29'N, 112°4'W

    _____

7. 32°42'N, 117°10'W

    _____

8. 40°47'N, 73°58'W

    _____

9. 45°24'N, 75°43'W

    _____

10. 49°13'N, 123°06'W

    _____

BONUS

Greek Gods and Goddesses

The ancient Greeks believed in many gods. The gods were mythical, not real, but played an important role in the lives of Greek men, women, and children. The hundreds of gods had different powers or abilities. Using the clues below, complete the crossword puzzle with the names of 13 gods and goddesses.

Across

3. Goddess of wisdom
4. God of thunder
5. Goddess of marriage
7. Goddess of agriculture
9. God of war
11. God of the sea
12. God of sleep

Down

1. God of the dead
2. God of commerce
3. Goddess of love
6. God of light and music
8. Goddess of the earth
10. God of time

World Landmarks

Write the correct number to identify each world landmark. Then, complete the table by writing the country where each landmark is located. Use reference resources if you need help.

Number	Landmark	Country
1	Great Wall of China	
2	Statue of Liberty	
3	Great Sphinx	
4	Taj Mahal	
5	Colosseum	
6	Stonehenge	
7	Eiffel Tower	
8	Chichén Itzá	

BONUS

Take It Outside!

Summer is a great time to explore your community. Brainstorm a list of five landmarks in your town, city, or county and identify these locations on a map. Then, invite your family and friends to join you on a landmark tour of your community. Bring a camera, a pen, and a notebook. At each landmark, take a group photo and ask each person for a comment about the landmark. After the tour, create a photo collage showing your friends and family at the landmarks along with their captioned comments.

With an adult, visit a local farmers' market. Bring a pen and a notebook and record the items that you observe for sale. Talk with the vendors about the things they are selling and the benefits of buying fresh produce. Once you are back home, review your notes and use them to create a 30-second commercial for the farmers' market. Record your commercial and share it with family, friends, and neighbors.

Go for a walk around your neighborhood with an adult. Take a pen and a notebook. Record the different types of animals you see, using tally marks to indicate multiple viewings of one type of animal. After your walk, review your notes. Then, show the results of your animal observation walk by creating a bar graph. Which animal did you find to be most prevalent in your neighborhood?

Visit a library or go online to locate more information about this animal. What sorts of habits does it have? Is it nocturnal or diurnal? What does it eat? What sort of predators does it have? When you have completed your research, write several informational paragraphs about the animal you chose. Share your writing via a letter or an e-mail with a friend who lives in a different town or state.

Monthly Goals

Think of three goals to set for yourself this month. For example, you may want to read for 30 minutes each day. Write your goals on the lines. Post them someplace visible, where you will see them every day.

Place a check mark next to each goal that you complete. Feel proud that you have met your goals and set new ones to continue to challenge yourself.

1. _____

2. _____

3. _____

Word List

The following words are used in this section. Use a dictionary to look up each word that you do not know. Then, write three sentences. Use at least one word from the word list in each sentence.

architecture   integrity

biome   molecules

constellation   pesticides

hieroglyphics   prospectors

incessant   Renaissance

1. _____

    _____

2. _____

    _____

3. _____

    _____

Introduction to Strength

This section includes fitness and character development activities that focus on strength. These activities are designed to get you moving and thinking about strengthening your body and your character. If you have limited mobility, feel free to modify any suggested exercises to fit your individual abilities.

Physical Strength

Like flexibility, strength is important for a healthy body. Many people think that a strong person is someone who can lift an enormous amount of weight. However, strength is more than the ability to pick up heavy barbells. Having strength is important for many everyday activities, such as helping with yardwork or lifting a younger sibling into a car seat. Muscular strength also helps reduce stress on your joints as your body ages.

Everyday activities and many fun exercises provide opportunities for you to build strength. Carrying bags of groceries, riding a bicycle, and swimming are all excellent ways to strengthen your muscles. Classic exercises, such as push-ups and chin-ups, are also fantastic strength builders.

Set realistic, achievable goals to improve your strength based on the activities you enjoy. Evaluate your progress during the summer months and, as you accomplish your strength goals, set new goals to challenge yourself.

Strength of Character

As you build your physical strength, work on your inner strength as well. Having a strong character means standing up for your beliefs, even if others do not agree with your viewpoint. Inner strength can be shown in many ways. For example, you can show inner strength by being honest, standing up for someone who needs your help, and putting your best effort into every task. It is not always easy to show inner strength. Think of a time when you showed inner strength, such as telling the truth when you broke your mother's favorite vase. How did you use your inner strength to handle that situation?

Use the summer months to develop a strong sense of self, both physically and emotionally. Celebrate your successes and look for ways to become even stronger. Reflect upon your accomplishments during the summer, and you will see positive growth on the inside as well as on the outside.

Find the volume of each rectangular prism. Give answers in simplest form.

1.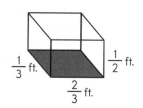
$\frac{1}{3}$ ft. $\frac{1}{2}$ ft. $\frac{2}{3}$ ft.

V = _____

2.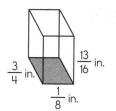
$\frac{3}{4}$ in. $\frac{13}{16}$ in. $\frac{1}{8}$ in.

V = _____

3.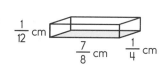
$\frac{1}{12}$ cm $\frac{7}{8}$ cm $\frac{1}{4}$ cm

V = _____

4.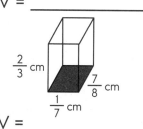
$\frac{2}{3}$ cm $\frac{7}{8}$ cm $\frac{1}{7}$ cm

V = _____

5.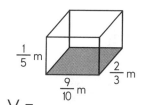
$\frac{1}{5}$ m $\frac{2}{3}$ m $\frac{9}{10}$ m

V = _____

6.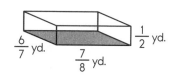
$\frac{6}{7}$ yd. $\frac{1}{2}$ yd. $\frac{7}{8}$ yd.

V = _____

Nonrestrictive elements appear inside commas, parentheses, or dashes to add additional information to a sentence. Rewrite each sentence including the nonrestrictive element.

7. Miller's Farm Stand has the best watermelons this time of year. (the one off of Route 82)

_____

8. We watched the ball soar and land on Mr. Wilson's deck. —right over the fence—

_____

9. My friend Emily taught me the funniest joke. , the girl I met at camp,

_____

10. After hiking all day, I fell asleep as soon as my head hit the pillow. —almost halfway up a mountain—

_____

11. Romana's has a special today on my favorite pizza. (mushroom, pepper, and bacon)

_____

12. *Escape From Space* was my favorite movie of the summer. (starring Ethan Myers)

_____

DAY 1

A *simile* is a comparison between two things that uses the word *like* or *as*. Read each sentence. Underline the simile and draw an arrow to what or who it is describing. Then, write what each simile means.

13. Mom did not feel well last week, but now she is as fit as a fiddle.

     _____

14. The detective had to be as smart as a fox to solve the mystery.

     _____

15. Her smile is like sunshine on a cloudy day.

     _____

16. His footsteps sounded like thunder on the wooden floor.

     _____

Write each fraction as a percentage. Write each percentage as a fraction in lowest terms.

17. $\frac{3}{5}$ =   18. $\frac{9}{10}$ =   19. $\frac{13}{100}$ =   20. $\frac{89}{100}$ =

21. 4% =   22. 16% =   23. 25% =   24. 34% =

FACTOID: Ostriches can run as fast as 40 miles (64.4 km) per hour.

DAY 2

Find the mean, median, mode, and range of each set of data.

1.   34, 41, 33, 41, 31

    mean: _____ median: _____

    mode: _____ range: _____

2.   18, 10, 10, 8, 35, 10, 21

    mean: _____ median: _____

    mode: _____ range: _____

3.   7, 14, 10, 14, 29, 16, 15

    mean: _____ median: _____

    mode: _____ range: _____

4.   41, 18, 24, 41, 72, 82, 16

    mean: _____ median: _____

    mode: _____ range: _____

Underline the whole verb phrase in each sentence. Circle each helping verb.

5.   The water is pouring into the basement.

6.   The rabbit had scurried into the hole.

7.   We are going to the amusement park.

8.   The lights can be dimmed with this switch.

9.   Max was taking his turn.

10.   The puppy must have tried to jump onto the bed.

11.   That jam would be good on toast.

12.   The bird had flown into the bushes.

13.   We should pull the weeds out of the garden.

14.   Asya may have been going to the zoo.

DAY 2

Read the passage. Then, answer the questions.

The Renaissance

Renaissance is a French word that means *rebirth*. Between AD 1350 and AD 1600, Europeans experienced a rebirth in the arts, literature, and science. In the Middle Ages, people forgot many of the ancient Greeks' and Romans' achievements because their daily lives were so hard. During the Renaissance, people began to reread ancient texts and create new art, literature, and architecture. One Renaissance author was William Shakespeare. His plays are still performed today. Many important Renaissance artists lived in Italy, including Michelangelo, Raphael, and Titian. The most famous figure of this period might be Leonardo da Vinci, who excelled in the areas of art, architecture, and science. Da Vinci's sketchbooks contain drawings of helicopters and airplanes, hundreds of years before they were even invented. When someone is referred to as a "Renaissance man" or a "Renaissance woman," it means that the person is good at many different things, like Leonardo da Vinci.

15. What is the main idea of this passage?
    A. During the Renaissance, people created new art forms.
    B. Many people learned to paint during the Renaissance.
    C. The Renaissance was an important time for science, literature, and the arts.

16. How long did the Renaissance last? _____

17. What happened during the Renaissance? _____
_____

18. How can you tell that Shakespeare was a great writer? _____
_____

19. In which areas did Leonardo da Vinci excel?_____
_____

20. What sort of connotation does the term *Renaissance man* or *Renaissance woman* have?

_____

FITNESS FLASH: Do five push-ups.

* See page ii.

Solve each problem. Write each improper fraction as a simplified mixed number.

1. $\frac{7}{2} \div \frac{1}{2} =$

2. $\frac{4}{3} \div \frac{2}{3} =$

3. $\frac{6}{4} \div \frac{3}{4} =$

4. $\frac{9}{2} \div \frac{1}{3} =$

5. $\frac{8}{3} \div \frac{2}{5} =$

6. $\frac{15}{4} \div \frac{3}{7} =$

7. $\frac{5}{6} \div \frac{5}{6} =$

8. $\frac{3}{8} \div \frac{3}{4} =$

9. $\frac{3}{4} \div \frac{5}{2} =$

The subject of a passive-voice sentence is acted upon. The subject of an active-voice sentence performs the action. Rewrite each sentence in the active voice.

10. Experiments have been conducted by students to test the hypothesis.

_____

11. The exam was passed by more than two-thirds of the applicants.

_____

12. The song is sung by the choir at every graduation.

_____

13. The vegetarian pizza was enjoyed by all of my friends.

_____

14. The nail was hammered into the wall by Cameron.

_____

DAY 3

A *metaphor* is a comparison between two things that does not use the word *like* or *as*. Read each sentence. Underline the two things that are being compared. Then, write what each metaphor means.

15. That test was a piece of cake.

     _____

16. Winning the award was a dream come true.

     _____

17. Our backyard was a blanket of snow.

     _____

18. My pillow was a cloud after the long day.

     _____

19. The lake was a mirror surrounded by tall, old trees.

     _____

Find the percentage of each number.

20. 3% of 10 =   21. 4% of 30 =   22. 16% of 80 =

23. 18% of 36 =   24. 6% of 80 =   25. 9% of 90 =

26. 8% of 68 =   27. 9% of 75 =   28. 62% of 62 =

29. 4% of 400 =   30. 3% of 200 =   31. 37% of 51 =

FACTOID: An elephant seal can dive 5,000 feet (1.52 km) underwater while searching for food.

Complete the table.

	Regular Price	Discount Rate	Discount	Sale Price
1.	$58	40%		
2.	$128	30%		
3.	$16	15%		
4.	$760	60%		
5.	$19	55%		
6.	$100	45%		
7.	$2,500	25%		

Draw a line through each incorrect verb. Then, write the correct verb above each crossed-out verb.

Game Day

Once a month, our school hold a game day in the gymnasium. We participate in races and other games. Fernando and Melvin always races on the same team. They enjoys running. Target toss is a favorite event. Each player toss the ball at a target painted on the wall. Laura and Jordana usually win because they practices after school. José and Luke like basketball. Kyle and Spencer usually scores more points, but José and Luke is improving all of the time. At the end of the day, two teams play a game of volleyball.

DAY 4

Read each analogy. On the line, write a label from the box that describes the relationship between the word pairs.

8. mast : sailboat :: transmission : car

_____

cause/effect

part/whole

item/category

9. joke : laughter :: tragedy : sadness

_____

10. lemonade : beverage :: willow : tree

_____

11. democracy : government :: hockey : sport

_____

12. digestive system : body :: troposphere : atmosphere

_____

13. nap : refreshed :: eat : nourished

_____

Wall Push-Ups

Strong muscles and bones are important for fitness and overall health. This exercise will help strengthen your arms, shoulders, and back. You will need three to four feet (0.9–1.2 m) of empty wall space and a few minutes each day, and soon you will reap the benefits of a stronger body.

This exercise is like doing a push-up against a wall instead of on the floor. To begin, stand straight and face the wall. Place your hands shoulder-width apart against the wall with your fingers pointing up. You should be standing far enough away from the wall that your elbows are only slightly bent.

As you inhale, bend your elbows and bring your face toward the wall. Exhale and push against the wall, straightening your arms until you have returned to the starting position. Remember to keep your body straight. Keep your heels as close to the floor as you can. Do two sets of 8–10 repetitions. For a challenge, try moving your hands farther apart or rotate your palms so that your fingers face slightly inward or outward.

* See page ii.

Solve each problem. Write each improper fraction as a simplified mixed number.

1. $11\frac{1}{2} \div 2\frac{7}{8} =$

2. $3\frac{1}{2} \div 2 =$

3. $4\frac{1}{4} \div 3\frac{1}{8} =$

4. $3\frac{3}{4} \div 5 =$

5. $3\frac{1}{2} \div 1\frac{3}{4} =$

6. $6\frac{1}{3} \div 2 =$

7. $8 \div 1\frac{1}{5} =$

8. $12\frac{3}{8} \div 2\frac{3}{4} =$

9. $5\frac{3}{5} \div 4\frac{2}{3} =$

A *direct object* is the noun or pronoun that receives the action of a verb and tells *who* or *what*. Underline the verb in each sentence. Circle each direct object.

10. The courtyard fountain continuously gushed water.

11. Leona frequently chews gum.

12. The anxious horse kicked the stall door.

13. Erica handed Jacob her paper.

14. Rochelle stowed the luggage in the overhead bin.

15. Danielle offered her carrots to Jesse.

16. Rosa canceled her subscription to the magazine.

17. Yolanda crochets one blanket each month.

18. Debbie made vegetable soup for dinner.

19. Enrique toasted a marshmallow over the campfire.

DAY 5

Read the passage. Then, answer the questions.

Rachel Carson

After World War II, farmers began using pesticides, such as DDT, to protect their crops. Near the farmlands where the pesticides were used, birds and animals were dying. Scientist Rachel Carson felt that she had to do something. She wrote a book in 1962 titled *Silent Spring* that described forests that were quiet and land that was dying.

Carson loved the outdoors, and she studied wildlife and marine biology in school. She worked as a scientist for the government and also wrote about natural history. Soon, she was in charge of all of the writing done by the U.S. Fish and Wildlife Service.

In 1941, Carson published her first book, *Under the Sea-Wind*. She published her second book, *The Sea Around Us*, in 1951. In 1955, she published a third book, *The Edge of the Sea*. Carson described life on the seashore and the animals and plants that lived in the oceans. Her books became national best sellers.

Then, Carson learned that she was seriously ill with cancer. At the same time, she began reading reports about DDT. Carson feared that she did not have a lot of time left to help. She wanted to keep writing about the sea, but she felt that it was more important to keep **toxic** chemicals away from crops and animals.

Silent Spring's publication caused a storm of argument about chemicals. The chemical companies said that the book was inaccurate, but Carson was certain that DDT was toxic. She spoke before the U.S. Congress, asking for new laws to protect the environment. President John F. Kennedy formed a committee to study the issue, and the committee confirmed the results of Carson's research. Congress passed laws about the use of DDT and the testing of other chemicals.

Carson died two years later. But, her work is still remembered, and efforts to protect the living world from chemicals and other dangers continue.

20. What does the word *toxic* mean? _____

21. What made Rachel Carson stop writing about the sea? _____

_____

_____

22. What did Carson study in school? _____

> **CHARACTER CHECK:** Make a list of at least three ways you can show patience at home. Share the list with a family member.

Rather than interpreting data, create data to fit the conditions described in each situation. Show your work to prove that you have chosen valid data.

1. Create a set of data that contains 11 test scores and satisfies each condition below:

   Mean: 83

   Median: 81

   Mode: 80

   Range: 26

2. Create a set of data that shows temperature highs for 10 days and satisfies each condition below:

   Mean: 72°

   Median: 74°

   Mode: 68°

   Range: 21°

An *indirect object* precedes the direct object in a sentence and tells *to whom* or *for whom* the action of the verb is done. Underline the verb in each sentence. Circle each indirect object.

3. José gave his puppy a bath.

4. Peter wished his grandmother a happy birthday.

5. Walter sold Yow the tire swing.

6. The waiter handed Kent his dinner plate.

7. Quinn offered Tommy her pencil.

8. Aunt May knitted June a yellow scarf.

9. Mr. Slider gave the chair a coat of varnish.

10. The students wrote their state representative a letter.

11. Our new neighbor brought our family some fresh vegetables.

DAY 6

Use the clue to unscramble each idiom. Write the idiom on the line.

12.   There can be many ways of doing something.
      lead roads Rome all to

      _____

13.   forced to decide between unpleasant choices
      and between hard rock a place a

      _____

14.   unable to think of a word that you know
      of the tongue on tip your

      _____

15.   to hear something and then immediately forget it
      the in out ear one other and

      _____

16.   to accept more responsibility than you can handle
      chew more bite than can you off

      _____

Pick one character in any book that you have read or movie that you have seen. Explain why you would want to be friends with this character. Use another sheet of paper if you need more space.

_____

_____

_____

_____

_____

_____

FACTOID: A lion's age can be estimated by the color of its nose.

Solve each problem.

1.
$$
\begin{array}{r}
2.8 \\
\times\ 34 \\
\hline
\end{array}
$$

2.
$$
\begin{array}{r}
6.2 \\
\times\ 13 \\
\hline
\end{array}
$$

3.
$$
\begin{array}{r}
3.7 \\
\times\ 65 \\
\hline
\end{array}
$$

4.
$$
\begin{array}{r}
0.17 \\
\times\ 14 \\
\hline
\end{array}
$$

5.
$$
\begin{array}{r}
0.52 \\
\times\ 26 \\
\hline
\end{array}
$$

6.
$$
\begin{array}{r}
0.208 \\
\times\ 21 \\
\hline
\end{array}
$$

7.
$$
\begin{array}{r}
302.6 \\
\times\ 83 \\
\hline
\end{array}
$$

8.
$$
\begin{array}{r}
3.208 \\
\times\ 91 \\
\hline
\end{array}
$$

9.
$$
\begin{array}{r}
0.43 \\
\times\ 18 \\
\hline
\end{array}
$$

10.
$$
\begin{array}{r}
0.618 \\
\times\ 36 \\
\hline
\end{array}
$$

11.
$$
\begin{array}{r}
214.4 \\
\times\ 17 \\
\hline
\end{array}
$$

12.
$$
\begin{array}{r}
4.197 \\
\times\ 43 \\
\hline
\end{array}
$$

Write each decimal as a percentage.

13. $0.37 =$

14. $0.69 =$

15. $0.40 =$

16. $0.21 =$

17. $0.999 =$

18. $0.499 =$

19. $1.75 =$

20. $2.25 =$

Write each percentage as a decimal.

21. $24\% =$

22. $65\% =$

23. $88\% =$

24. $3\% =$

25. $17\% =$

26. $9\% =$

27. $10\% =$

28. $86\% =$

DAY 7

Personification is a literary device in which an author gives human characteristics or emotions, such as love, to something that is not human, such as the moon. **Read each sentence and explain what is being personified.**

29. Fortune smiled on us that bright summer morning. _____

    _____

30. The clock in the tower sang the time to the townspeople. _____

    _____

31. The wind whistled cheerfully through the iron gates. _____

    _____

32. The daisies beside the road waved happily as I walked past them. _____

    _____

33. The Marino family will go to the zoo if the weather permits. _____

    _____

Find the area of each figure.

34.

    A = _____ cm²

35.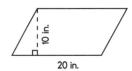

    A = _____ in.²

36.

    A = _____ ft.²

37.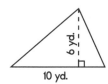

    A = _____ yd.²

38.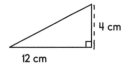

    A = _____ cm²

39.

    A = _____ cm²

FITNESS FLASH: Do 10 sit-ups.

* See page ii.

Solve each problem.

1. A covered wagon on the Oregon Trail could travel about 2.5 miles per hour on flat terrain. About how many miles could it travel in 9 hours?

2. In 1860, gingham cloth sold for $0.25 per yard. Mrs. Olsen bought 16.4 yards to make clothes for her whole family. How much did she spend on cloth?

3. In 1863 in Fort Laramie, Wyoming, travelers could buy beef jerky at the trading post for $0.35 per pound. How much would a 16-pound box of beef jerky cost?

4. Each wagon in the Parley Company of Travelers wagon train was about 3.65 meters long. If 12 wagons traveled end to end, how long would the wagon train be?

Write em dashes where they are needed in the paragraph.

Woeful Woofer

Woofer that silly dog is home again. I called actually, whistled for Woofer to come to dinner. Usually, he runs into the kitchen, but the house was quiet. I didn't know where he could be. I was searching for Woofer when Carol my older sister came home from school. When I told her that Woofer was missing, she helped me look in every room even under the beds. We couldn't find Woofer. Carol asked Mrs. Linden the retired teacher next door if she had seen him. Then, Nicholas Carol's friend walked up the street with Woofer trotting behind him.

DAY 8

Read the passage. Then, answer the questions.

First, the Lightning

Lightning is a powerful force of nature. The air around a single bolt of lightning is hotter than the surface of the sun. Although its formation is similar to a spark of static electricity, a lightning strike releases a tremendous amount of energy.

During a storm, small particles in clouds collect either positive or negative charges of energy. The lighter, positively charged particles rise to the top of the clouds. The heavier, negatively charged particles fall to the bottom of the clouds. This separation creates a path through the air for the flow of electricity. Once the attraction between the two groups becomes too strong, the particles release their stored energy. This electrical discharge is lightning.

The thunder that follows lightning is the sound made by the air as the lightning heats it. Lightning can instantly heat air molecules to more than 50,000°F (27,760°C). These heated molecules then expand and collide. This explosion of air is the source of the sound waves that we call thunder.

Although it seems like lightning and thunder occur at different times, this is only a trick of the senses. Light travels much faster than sound. This difference in speed explains why lightning and thunder reach us at different times. The sound of thunder takes more time than the light from a lightning strike to travel the same distance.

5. What is the sound of thunder? _____

_____

6. Why do we see lightning first and hear thunder later?_____

_____

7. Which of these statements is true?
    A. A lightning strike can be as hot as 1,000,000°F (555,538°C).
    B. Light travels at one-fifth the speed of sound.
    C. Negatively charged particles rise to the top of a cloud.
    D. The air around a single bolt of lightning is hotter than the surface of the sun.

8. What is the main difference between a lightning strike and static electricity?

_____

FACTOID: More than 35 million people live in and around Tokyo, Japan.

Solve each problem.

1. $2\overline{)45.4}$

2. $2\overline{)4.5}$

3. $7\overline{)34.37}$

4. $5\overline{)0.105}$

5. $6\overline{)120.6}$

6. $6\overline{)12.06}$

7. $4\overline{)2.44}$

8. $6\overline{)2.76}$

Students scored these points on a quiz: 9, 18, 12, 9, 13, 22, 8, 23, 16, 17, 22, 20, 22, 15, 10, 17, 21, 23, 14, 11. Use the data to complete the histogram. Then, answer the questions.

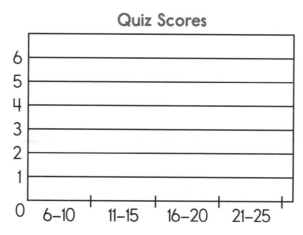

Quiz Scores

9. Find the measures of center and variability for the data.

mean: _____   range: _____

median: _____   mode: _____

10. What percentage of the students scored 16–20% _____

11. What percentage of the scores range from 21 to 25 points? _____

DAY 9

Write each literary term from the word bank on the line next to its definition.

allusion	conflict	dialogue
foreshadowing	hyperbole	imagery
irony	point of view	setting

12. _____ the struggle within the story

13. _____ a reference to a real or fictitious person, place, or event

14. _____ spoken conversation between two characters

15. _____ exaggeration for effect

16. _____ using hints or clues to suggest what might happen later in a story

17. _____ the perspective from which a story is told

18. _____ the time and place in which a story occurs

19. _____ the use of words that mean the opposite of what one intends

20. _____ the use of descriptive language to help readers form vivid mental pictures

Integrity means having sound moral principles and being honest. Read the situation. On a separate sheet of paper, write a possible consequence of not demonstrating integrity. Then, write a benefit received for showing integrity.

You are the catcher on a softball team that is in a big game. If you win, your team will be in first place. A player from the other team is sprinting toward home plate. The ball is thrown to you. You catch the ball but just miss tagging the player sliding into home. The umpire has a blocked view and hesitates for a moment before calling the other team's player out.

FITNESS FLASH: Do 10 squats.

* See page ii.

Solve each problem.

1. $0.6\overline{)5.4}$

2. $0.9\overline{)0.18}$

3. $1.4\overline{)13.86}$

4. $0.86\overline{)0.688}$

5. $1.7\overline{)10.54}$

6. $2.4\overline{)16.8}$

7. $0.07\overline{)0.035}$

8. $0.92\overline{)0.736}$

Rewrite each sentence, placing en dashes and em dashes where they are needed.

9. The appointments available are 12:00 P.M. 4:00 P.M.

_____

10. The assignment for tomorrow is to read pages 24 36 carefully.

_____

11. The Chicago New York flight lasts less than two hours.

_____

12. We go to great lengths often far beyond our normal limitations to win!

_____

13. If I only needed to read chapters 2 4, I would be finished by now.

_____

CHARACTER CHECK: Write five things that you are grateful for. Share your list with an adult.

DAY 10

Read the descriptions of waking up at Frog Pond. Then, answer the questions.

Camper One
We woke this morning to waves lapping the shore, a breeze rustling the leaves, and frogs croaking. They woke the geese and ducks, who sang good morning to the animals around the pond. Soon, all of the insects, birds, and animals were calling good morning to one another. How could I stay in bed? I needed to greet the morning, too.

Camper Two
We woke this morning to the incessant croaking of frogs. This triggered off-key honking and quacking from around the pond. Waves slapped the shore, and the wind roared through the trees. Soon, the insects, birds, and animals were loudly protesting the hour. With all of this noise, it was hardly worth trying to go back to sleep.

14. How does Camper One feel about waking up at Frog Pond? _____

_____

15. How does Camper Two feel about waking up at Frog Pond? _____

_____

16. Write two facts about what happened at Frog Pond that morning. _____

_____

_____

Circle the letter in front of the correct meaning for each affix. Then, write a word that contains the affix.

17. -ish   A. like   B. before   C. across   _____

18. anti-   A. after   B. more   C. against   _____

19. -hood   A. many   B. condition of   C. between   _____

20. sub-   A. above   B. before   C. below, under   _____

21. inter-   A. between, among B. not   C. against   _____

22. -ly   A. characteristic of B. opposite of   C. wrongly   _____

23. -en   A. cause to   B. opposite of   C. made of   _____

24. semi-   A. into   B. partly   C. again   _____

Find the unit rate in each problem. Equivalent ratios are provided for the first two problems. Solve for the variable.

1. A baker uses $3\frac{1}{4}$ cups of sugar in 8 batches of cookies. How much sugar is used in one batch of cookies? Let *a* represent the amount of sugar.

   equivalent ratios: $\dfrac{3\frac{1}{4}}{8} = \dfrac{a}{1}$ _____ cups of sugar in each batch

2. Stephan hiked $7\frac{2}{5}$ miles in 4 hours. How many miles did he hike per hour? Let *x* represent the number of miles.

   equivalent ratios: $\dfrac{7\frac{2}{5}}{4} = \dfrac{x}{1}$ _____ miles each hour

3. A hose pumped $118\frac{1}{8}$ gallons of water from a pool in 15 minutes. How much water did the hose pump each minute? Let *y* represent the number of gallons.

   equivalent ratios: _____ gallons each minute

A *modifier* is a word or phrase that describes a noun or pronoun. In sentences with a *dangling modifier*, it is unclear what the modifier is describing. Rewrite each sentence so that it is clear what the modifier is describing.

EXAMPLE: Covered with mud, I saw the puppy running across the yard.
   I saw the puppy, who was covered with mud, running across the yard.

4. While putting on my pajamas, my sister fell asleep.

   _____

5. Laughing at the show on TV, my glass of milk spilled.

   _____

6. While walking to school, a tiny, mewing kitten caught my attention.

   _____

7. After a quick change of clothes, Mom told me to set the table for dinner.

   _____

8. Though only 4 years old, Megan taught her sister to read.

   _____

DAY 11

Read the passage. Then, answer the questions.

from *Little Men* by Louisa May Alcott

The house seemed swarming with boys, who were beguiling the rainy twilight with all sorts of amusements. There were boys everywhere, "up-stairs and down-stairs and in the lady's chamber," apparently, for various open doors showed pleasant groups of big boys, little boys, and middle-sized boys in all stages of evening relaxation, not to say effervescence. Two large rooms on the right were evidently schoolrooms, for desks, maps, blackboards, and books were scattered about. An open fire burned on the hearth, and several indolent lads lay on their backs before it, discussing a new cricket-ground, with such animation that their boots waved in the air. A tall youth was practising on the flute in one corner, quite undisturbed by the racket all about him. Two or three others were jumping over the desks, pausing, now and then, to get their breath and laugh at the droll sketches of a little wag who was caricaturing the whole household on a blackboard.

In the room on the left a long supper-table was seen, set forth with great pitchers of new milk, piles of brown and white bread, and perfect stacks of the shiny gingerbread so dear to boyish souls. A flavor of toast was in the air, also suggestions of baked apples, very **tantalizing** to one hungry little nose and stomach.

The hall, however, presented the most inviting prospect of all, for a brisk game of tag was going on in the upper entry. One landing was devoted to marbles, the other to checkers, while the stairs were occupied by a boy reading, a girl singing a lullaby to her doll, two puppies, a kitten, and a constant succession of small boys sliding down the banisters, to the great detriment of their clothes and danger to their limbs.

9. From whose point of view do you think this selection is told? Why?_____

_____

10. When do you think this story takes place? Explain._____

_____

11. How does the author's description of the scene create a vivid setting for the story? _____

_____

12. Use the context of the sentence to define the word *tantalizing*. _____

_____

Using the number line below, draw a box-and-whisker plot for the following data:
12, 18, 18, 20, 22, 22, 25, 26, 30, 30, 32, 32, 35, 35, 38, 40, 42.

1.   What is the median score?_____

2.   What is the lower quartile?_____

3.   What is the upper quartile? _____

0   5   10   15   20   25   30   35   40   45   50

Draw a line through each incorrect adverb. Write the correct adverb above each incorrect word.

Motion on the Moon

On August 2, 1971, Commander David R. Scott stood proud on the surface of the moon.

As the cameras rolled, the astronaut dramatic dropped a feather and a hammer.

On Earth, the hammer would fall much fast. Amazing, the two objects landed on the

moon's surface at the same time. Unbelievable, Galileo Galilei had accurate predicted

the results of this experiment near 400 years earlier. A legend claims that Galileo bold

dropped a cannonball and a musket ball from the Leaning Tower of Pisa in Pisa, Italy, to

test his theory, but few modern historians actual believe the tale.

DAY 12

Identify the setting in each situation. Write the place and circle the time.

4. Heath studies the *Tyrannosaurus rex* display at The Field Museum in Chicago, Illinois, and writes several answers on his field trip questionnaire.

    Where? _____

    When?   in the past   in the present   in the future

5. Jill was exhausted. She woke at sunup to cook breakfast over the campfire and load the wagon. Then, she got in line with the other wagons. Eight hours later, she was still sitting on the buckboard, trying to guide the oxen. She hoped that the place called California was worth the three-month trip.

    Where? _____

    When?   in the past   in the present   in the future

6. Luis sat at his desk. He was bored. He had heard the history lesson about the wars of the 1900s many times. After all, they happened more than 600 years ago.

    Where? _____

    When?   in the past   in the present   in the future

What is one talent or skill that you possess? How can you develop it into a career? Use another sheet of paper if you need more space.

_____

_____

_____

_____

_____

_____

_____

_____

FITNESS FLASH: Do five push-ups.

* See page ii.

Solve. Write fractions in simplest form.

1. $-12 + 8 =$ _____

2. $25 - (-4) =$ _____

3. $-8 - 3 =$ _____

4. $13 + (-5) =$ _____

5. $-4 + (-9) =$ _____

6. $-15 - 6 =$ _____

7. $\frac{1}{9} + 3\frac{5}{8} =$ _____

8. $1\frac{5}{6} - \frac{3}{4} =$ _____

9. $4\frac{3}{7} + 2\frac{1}{2} =$ _____

10. $1\frac{2}{3} + 3\frac{2}{9} =$ _____

11. $5\frac{7}{12} - 3\frac{3}{5} =$ _____

12. $8\frac{3}{4} - 4\frac{5}{7} =$ _____

Write *I* beside each independent clause. Write *D* beside each dependent clause.

13. _____ When Sonya arrived at her dance class

14. _____ Nazir was not worried about giving his presentation on Tuesday

15. _____ I hope that Ms. Oh does not need surgery on her ankle

16. _____ Because Laura hates watching scary movies

17. _____ I plan to be a veterinarian or a geologist

18. _____ If you forget your lunch again

A *complex sentence* includes an independent clause and one or more dependent clauses. Underline each independent clause once and each dependent clause twice.

19. Lena wrapped the gifts and hid them before her mom came home.

20. Boseley raced across the yard, hoping to finally catch the pesky squirrel.

21. Samantha made it to the regional spelling bee because she studied hard for months.

22. On the first Thursday of every month, our book group meets for snacks and a discussion of our latest book.

23. Although we forgot to hang our food from a tree, the bears and raccoons did not raid our campsite overnight.

DAY 13

You can help preserve the environment around you. In the *cause* column of the chart, read how people have helped plants and animals. In the *effect* column, write how each cause helped the local environment.

Cause	Effect
Milkweed grows in a field but will be destroyed this winter when houses are built. Monarch butterflies lay their eggs on milkweed plants, and monarch caterpillars eat the plants. In the fall, Judy gathered some milkweed seeds. She got her parents' permission to plant the seeds in their backyard.	
David and his dad were canoeing in the creek. David saw a bird caught in a net on the shore. He and his dad rescued the bird and took it to a veterinarian. The veterinarian removed the bird from the net and threw the net in the trash.	

"Step-Up" to Fitness

A "step-up" is a strength exercise that uses the weight of your body to strengthen the hamstrings and quadriceps, two large muscle groups in your legs. For this exercise, you will need a sturdy, low footstool and a few minutes three or four days a week.

Stand in front of your footstool. Place your right foot firmly on the footstool. Push through your right foot to lift your body onto the footstool. Stand with both feet on the footstool. Then, leading with your right foot, carefully step down to the starting position. Keep your back straight and your abdominal muscles tight. Switch feet and repeat the exercise. Do two sets of 8–10 repetitions for each leg.

FACTOID: An adult human's intestines are about 20 feet (6.1 m) long.

* See page ii.

Use the given probability to predict long-term outcomes. Round answers to the nearest whole number.

1. The probability of pulling a green marble out of bag of colored marbles is 2:5. If you were to pull colored marbles out of the bag (one at a time, and putting the marble back each time) for 600 tries, approximately how many times would you select a green marble? _____ times

2. The probability of spinning a 4 on a spinner is 0.125. If you spun 150 times, approximately how many times would the spinner land on 4? _____ times

3. The probability of drawing a queen of hearts from a deck of cards is $\frac{1}{52}$. If you drew one card at a time (and put the card back each time) for 300 tries, how many times total could you expect to draw a queen of hearts? _____ times

A *gerund* is a verb that ends in *-ing* and is used as a noun. Underline the gerund phrase in each sentence below.

4. Skiing and hiking are the after-school activities that Antonio likes best.

5. Saving his money is important to Colin, because he wants to buy a new game.

6. Lizette knows that taking piano and voice lessons requires a large time commitment.

7. Cleaning out the chicken coop is not one of Micah's favorite chores.

8. On Saturday mornings, Alyssa's main priority is cleaning her room.

An *infinitive* is a verb form in which *to* is followed by the base form of the verb. Underline the infinitive phrase in each sentence below.

9. Ms. Greenbaum said that all she wants is for us each to achieve our personal best.

10. Katie tried to stop the leak, but it was too late.

11. Zara hopes to impress her parents with the painting in the student art show.

12. To be a good listener is an important and valuable character trait.

13. Uncle Scott asked us to weed the garden before lunch.

Read the passage. Then, answer the questions.

The Klondike Gold Rush

The Klondike Gold Rush was named after a river where a large deposit of gold was found in 1896. The Klondike River is located near Dawson City in Canada's Yukon Territory. People who wanted to travel from Alaska to Canada in search of gold had to bring one year's worth of supplies with them because there were no places along the way to get more supplies. They often spent time in Edmonton, Canada, stocking up on food, tools, and clothing for the journey.

The gold rush helped develop new towns in western Canada and the Pacific Northwest of the United States. In addition to thousands of prospectors, or people who searched for gold, the gold rush drew many professionals, such as doctors and teachers, who were needed in the new settlements. Today, the Klondike Gold Rush International Historical Park, which includes sites in both Canada and the United States, helps people remember the dreams of the prospectors and the difficulties they faced.

14. What was the Klondike Gold Rush named after? _____

_____

15. What did people need to bring with them when traveling from Alaska to Canada?

_____

_____

16. What did people often do in Edmonton? _____

_____

17. Where did new towns develop during the gold rush?_____

_____

18. Visit the library or go online to find another piece of writing about the Klondike Gold Rush. If possible, search for a firsthand or eyewitness account. How is the information you find similar to and different from the information in this passage? Use a separate sheet of paper for your answer.

FITNESS FLASH: Do 10 lunges.

* See page ii.

Add each pair of expressions.

1. $3x + 7$ and $x + 4$ _____

2. $y - 5$ and $2y + 6$ _____

3. $5a + 3$ and $-3a + 1$ _____

Subtract the second expression from the first expression.

4. $5x + 7$ minus $2x + 2$ _____

5. $7y - 2$ minus $y + 4$ _____

6. $b + 8$ minus $-2b + 5$ _____

Factor each expression.

7. $12y - 3$ _____

8. $4x^2 - 12x$ _____

9. $-9c + 3$ _____

Write a sentence for each word below. The words in each pair have similar denotations but different connotations.

10. lost _____

    misplaced _____

11. unique _____

    odd _____

12. odor _____

    aroma _____

13. stare _____

    glower _____

14. pushy _____

    confident _____

DAY 15

Read the paragraph. Then, answer the questions.

Stars and Planets

Stars and planets are types of objects in outer space. They are far from Earth and look like bright specks in the night sky. A planet can be solid or made of gas, but a star is a ball of hot gases. Planets absorb light from the sun, while stars produce their own light. Stars are extremely hot, but planets can be any temperature.

15. What two things does this paragraph compare? _____

16. How are the two things similar? How are they different? _____

_____

_____

Write the letter of each biome from the word bank next to its description. You will use some biomes more than once.

| A. deciduous forest | B. desert | C. grassland |
| D. taiga | E. tropical rain forest | F. tundra |

17. _____ has the largest diversity of animal and plant life

18. _____ has evergreen trees that can stand cold temperatures

19. _____ has a canopy of trees that lets little light reach the understory

20. _____ has many types of deciduous trees

21. _____ has animals, such as hawks, deer, moose, and wolves

22. _____ has very little rainfall

23. _____ has animals, such as zebras, lions, rhinoceroses, and owls

24. _____ has animals, such as insects, spiders, reptiles, and birds

25. _____ has tall grasses that provide food and shelter for animals

26. _____ has animals, such as squirrels, rabbits, wolves, and bears

27. _____ has permafrost that is frozen year-round

CHARACTER CHECK: Look up the word *reliable* in a dictionary. How are you reliable?

Solve each word problem.

1. The length of one side of a cube is 8 cm.

   What is the cube's surface area? _____ cm²

   What is the cube's volume? _____ cm³

2. A state park is 16.5 miles long and 8.3 miles wide. Assuming the park's shape is rectangular, what is its area? _____ square miles

3. Malcolm built a toy box for his younger sister. It is 24 inches tall, 36 inches wide, and 18 inches deep. What is the volume of the toy box? _____ in.³

   Malcolm wants to paint the outside of the toy box. If each can of paint covers 10 square feet, how many cans will he need to buy? _____ cans of paint

4. A triangular traffic sign has a height of 45 cm. It is 75 cm long at its base. What is the area of the sign? _____ cm²

5. A square pyramid has a height of 12 feet. Each side of the base is 7 feet long. Use the following formula to calculate the pyramid's volume: $V = \frac{1}{3}(s^2 \times h)$.

   _____ ft.³

Match each root word in the first column with its meaning in the second column. Use a dictionary if you need help.

auto as in *automobile*	see
spec as in *spectacles*	one
ped as in *pedal*	foot
aqua as in *aquarium*	write
ject as in *reject*	throw
scrib/script as in *manuscript*	carry
port as in *transport*	water
mono as in *monarchy*	self

Read the paragraph. Then, answer the questions.

Biographies and Mysteries

Biographies and mysteries are both types of books. A biography contains facts about a person's life. It might be written by that person or by someone else. A mystery is usually fictional. It describes how a puzzle or problem is solved by a detective, a police officer, or another person.

6. What two things does this paragraph compare? _____

7. How are the two things similar? How are they different? _____

_____

Read the passage. Draw a line to match each of the statue's features with its meaning.

The Statue of Liberty

In 1884, France gave the United States a statue named *Liberty Enlightening the World*. The statue celebrated the spirit of liberty and the friendship between the two countries. It stands near the former immigration station at Ellis Island, where it greeted millions of immigrants who entered the United States. The statue became known as the Statue of Liberty, and it has come to represent freedom and opportunity.

The statue stands on Liberty Island in New York City, New York. It was originally designed to serve as a lighthouse. However, when the torch was lit, its light was too dim to see from far away. After a renovation in 1986, the torch was rebuilt and covered in gold leaf.

8. broken chain at her feet

9. crown with seven spikes

10. shining torch

11. flowing robe

12. July IV, MDCCLXXVI on the tablet

13. tablet in the shape of a keystone

A. the light of liberty

B. seven seas and continents

C. the Roman goddess of liberty

D. breaking free from tyranny

E. book of law that holds everything together

F. date the Declaration of Independence was signed

> **FACTOID:** Most of Indonesia's approximately 13,000 islands are uninhabited by people.

Determine the probability that each event will happen. Simplify if possible.

A jar contains 18 marbles that are all the same size. It contains 7 purple marbles, 3 green marbles, and 8 orange marbles. Without looking, Travis chooses 1 marble. What is the probability of each of the following outcomes?

1. P(green) = ____
2. P(not green) = ____
3. P(purple) = ____
4. P(purple or green) = ____
5. P(orange) = ____
6. P(not orange) = ____

Determine the probability that each event will happen. Simplify if possible.

A die numbered 1 through 6 is rolled. Find the probability of each outcome.

7. P(5) = ____
8. P(1 or 2) = ____
9. P(odd number) = ____
10. P(not 6) = ____
11. P(even number) = ____
12. P(1, 2, 3, or 4) = ____

An *allusion* is a reference to a person, place, or thing from history, literature, or mythology. Find and underline the allusion in each sentence below. On the line that follows, explain what the allusion means.

13. Mrs. Pizzarelli asked Cameron to stop acting like such a Romeo around the girls.

    _____

14. Clare asked more and more questions about the surprise, but her mother cautioned her not to open a Pandora's box.

    _____

15. Diego had been working out for months before the competition, and he finally felt like a real-life Hercules.

    _____

16. "Devon is such an Einstein," said Gabriella. "He didn't miss a single question on the science test!"

    _____

17. Maggie, who rarely believed anything her brother said, half expected Peter's nose to start growing like Pinocchio's.

    _____

DAY 17

Read the passage. Then, answer the questions.

The Rosetta Stone

The Rosetta Stone was found among ruins in Egypt more than 200 years ago. It unlocked the mystery of the symbols that cover the temples and tombs of Ancient Egypt. The Rosetta Stone was carved and displayed for people to read in approximately 196 BC. It was named after the place where it was found, a town called Rosetta in what is today the country of Egypt.

There are three different kinds of writing on the stone. The writing on the top part of the stone consists of rows of small pictures, called *hieroglyphics*. Hieroglyphics were often carved on walls or on slabs of stone. The Egyptian priests used hieroglyphics. The second kind of writing on the stone is now known as **demotic**, or popular, script. It was used by the Greeks in their everyday writing—for example, to send messages. The third section, located at the bottom of the stone, is written in Greek. By 196 BC, a Greek family named the Ptolemys had been ruling Egypt for over 100 years. Because of this, the Greek alphabet and language were being used in Egypt along with Egyptian writing.

18. What is the main idea of the first paragraph?_____
_____
_____

19. What is the main idea of the second paragraph? _____
_____
_____

20. What is the main idea of the entire passage?_____
_____
_____

21. Which of the following best defines the word *demotic*?
    A. angry
    C. written in stone
    B. popular
    D. language

FITNESS FLASH: Do 10 squats.

* See page ii.

84

Continue each number pattern.

1. 5, 8, 11, 14, 17, ____ , ____ , ____

2. 91, 86, 81, 76, 71, ____ , ____ , ____

3. 100, 92, 84, 76, 68, ____ , ____ , ____

4. 10, 20, 25, 35, 40, ____ , ____ , ____

5. 72, 69, 66, 63, 60, ____ , ____ , ____

6. 317, 402, 487, 572, ____ , ____ , ____

7. 5, 11, 23, 41, 65, ____ , ____ , ____

8. 244, 226, 208, 190, ____ , ____ , ____

9. 1, 4, 9, 16, 25, ____ , ____ , ____

10. 1, 2, 4, 8, 16, ____ , ____ , ____

Write the part of speech of each boldfaced word.

11. The roof **on** the old barn is peeling. _____

12. A row of ants **marched** across the picnic blanket. _____

13. My **stepmom** loves to visit Montreal, Quebec. _____

14. Walter put on his boots before going **outside**. _____

15. Taylor and her parents are driving to **Oregon**. _____

16. Evan wants to visit France, **and** Brianna wants to visit Italy. _____

17. Samantha bought **three** peaches at the store. _____

18. Kobe often **eats** lunch with his friend Victoria. _____

19. Is **he** going to the store with Jamil? _____

20. **The** dance will take place in the school gym. _____

DAY 18

Read each sentence. If the sentence contains faulty reasoning, explain why the reasoning is illogical. If it does not contain faulty reasoning, write *logical*.

21. Children over the age of 12 were admitted, so Ashley, age 13, and Bryan, age 14, were allowed in, while Fern, age 6, would have to wait. _____

_____

22. Every time I carry a green and purple umbrella, it rains. Therefore, if I carry a green and purple umbrella tomorrow, it will rain. _____

_____

23. Lamar waters his lawn on even-numbered days. So, on odd-numbered days, he keeps his sprinklers off. _____

_____

Write the letter of each type of renewable energy next to its description.

A. biomass	B. geothermal	C. hydroelectric
D. solar	E. tidal	F. wind

24. _____ uses the steam and hot water produced by energy within Earth to operate power plants and heat homes

25. _____ burns organic material from plants to produce steam for making electricity or heating homes; can also be made into automobile fuel

26. _____ uses the daily rising and falling of ocean levels to power turbines that spin a generator to create electricity

27. _____ directs flowing water through a turbine that spins a generator to create electricity

28. _____ photovoltaic cells convert the sun's radiation into usable electricity

29. _____ fast-moving air turns turbines that spin a generator to create electricity

FACTOID: There are more than 900 species of bats in the world.

Solve each problem.

1. In a sample, 11 out of 25 marbles are green. Predict approximately how many green marbles are in a box of 100 marbles.

2. In a sample, 54 out of 75 middle school students said that they are going to the school carnival. Based on this sample, approximately how many of the 750 middle school students are going to the carnival?

3. In a sample of 50 sixth-grade students, 32 students said that they are entering the school writing contest. Based on this sample, approximately how many of the school's 250 sixth graders will enter the writing contest?

4. In a sample, 25 sixth graders reported their T-shirt sizes. The results were: small–3, medium–9, and large–13. Approximately how many of each size should be ordered for 250 sixth graders?

There is a misplaced modifier in each sentence. Rewrite the sentences, moving the modifiers to the correct places.

EXAMPLE: I liked the striped boy's sweater.
I liked the boy's striped sweater.

5. My sisters stood in line to buy tickets for the concert for 45 minutes.

_____

6. Eli made the muffins for his mom with a lemon glaze.

_____

7. The art teacher said on Thursday that she would return our projects.

_____

8. The gorgeous girl's photograph won first place in the show.

_____

DAY 19

Read each question and evaluate how you would answer it. Use the key to write the level of your answer on the line.

Level 1 = yes or no response   Level 2 = one-word or short answer   Level 3 = extended answer

9. _____ Where is the Grand Canyon?

10. _____ How does a virus invade the body?

11. _____ How do you make chocolate chip cookies?

12. _____ Where do anemones live?

13. _____ Do people float in space?

14. _____ How is energy delivered from the dam to houses?

15. _____ What is the name of the winning football team?

16. _____ How does a spider make a web?

17. _____ When do monarch butterflies migrate?

18. _____ Do cheetahs run faster than gazelles?

19. _____ When is soccer season?

20. _____ Will you study for the test with me?

You have been offered a round-trip ride in a time machine and can travel any distance into the past. What time period would you want to travel to? Why? Use another sheet of paper if you need more space.

_____

_____

_____

_____

_____

FITNESS FLASH: Do 10 sit-ups.

* See page ii.

In descending order, list the four rules that apply to the order of operations.

_____

_____

_____

_____

Use the order of operations to simplify each math expression. Then, solve each equation.

1. $28 \div 7 + 10 =$ _____

2. $6 \times 2 + 6 \times 3 =$ _____

3. $40 - 3 \times 4 + 5 =$ _____

4. $(10 - 4) \times 3 - 10 =$ _____

5. $9 + 6 - 12 + 8 =$ _____

6. $(7 + 2) \div (7 - 4) =$ _____

Write *I* if the group of words is an independent clause. Write *D* if the group of words is a dependent clause.

7. _____ whenever Dillon receives a letter

8. _____ everyone encourages him

9. _____ Martina rides her horse, Tally

10. _____ so Chad bought a new hat

11. _____ those flowers are blooming early

12. _____ until Lila finishes her homework

13. _____ I walked one mile before school

14. _____ since it was lightning and thundering

DAY 20

Read the passage. Then, answer the questions.

Constellations

Constellations are patterns of stars that are visible in the night sky. Some constellations are named after animals, and others are named after mythical characters. Although stars in a constellation may look close together, they are actually very far apart. Brighter stars are closer to Earth, and dimmer stars are farther away.

The International Astronomical Union (IAU) recognizes 88 official constellations. One of the best-known constellations is the Big Dipper. The stars appear to form the handle and bowl of a water dipper. The Big Dipper is part of a larger constellation known as Ursa Major, or the Great Bear.

People in different parts of the world see different parts of the night sky. Different constellations are also visible at different times of the year. However, some constellations can be seen by people in both hemispheres. The constellation of Orion, the Hunter, is visible in both the Northern and Southern Hemispheres, but in the Southern Hemisphere, it appears upside down!

15.   What is the main idea of this passage?
   A.   Constellations are patterns of stars that are present in the night sky.
   B.   Some stars are very far from Earth.
   C.   Australia is located in the Southern Hemisphere.

16.   What are constellations named for? _____

_____

17.   Why do some stars appear brighter than others?

_____

_____

18.   What is the IAU? _____

19.   Ancient civilizations created myths and legends to explain the constellations they saw in the night sky. Do some research about these stories. Choose one and write a summary of it on a separate sheet of paper.

CHARACTER CHECK: Keep a tally through the day of the number of times you show consideration. Share the results with a family member.

Bending Light

How is light refracted, or bent, as it passes through transparent objects, such as glass and water?

Materials:
- coins, pebbles, and similar small objects that sink
- clear drinking glass filled with water
- flashlight
- masking tape
- pencil
- sharpened pencil
- small aquarium or clear rectangular container

Procedure:
Place the pencil in the glass of water and observe it from different angles. Then, fill the aquarium or clear rectangular container with water. Place various objects that sink, such as coins or pebbles, in the water. Look at these objects from the side, from above, and at an angle. Cover the front of the flashlight with several layers of masking tape. Poke a hole near the center of the tape with the sharpened pencil. When you turn on the flashlight, a thin beam of light should shine through the hole. Turn off the lights in the room. Focus the light into the aquarium from the side, from above, and at different angles.

1. Describe what you saw when you observed the pencil in the glass of water.

   _____

   _____

   _____

2. Describe what you saw when you looked at the coins, pebbles, or other objects in the aquarium from the side, from above, and at different angles. _____

   _____

   _____

3. Describe what you saw when you shone the light into the aquarium from the side, from above, and at different angles. _____

   _____

   _____

BONUS

Lifting with Air!

Is air pressure strong enough to lift heavy objects?

Even though gases like oxygen and carbon dioxide are invisible, they still exert pressure on objects around them. In this activity, you will test the strength of air pressure.

Materials:
- 1-gallon resealable plastic bag
- 3–4 books
- duct or packaging tape
- plastic drinking straw
- sharpened pencil

Procedure:
Seal the plastic bag. Place one book on top of the bag and leave about 2" (5 cm) of the bottom of the bag showing beneath the book. Use the sharpened pencil to poke a hole in the bag. Place the drinking straw in the hole. Use the tape to seal the space around the straw so that no air can escape. Blow into the straw. When you need to take a breath, place your finger over the end of the straw to keep air from leaking out. Blow into the bag until it is partially inflated. Observe what happens to the book when you blow into the bag. Then, place two or three books on top of the first book and continue to blow into the straw.

1. What happened to the book when you blew into the bag? _____

_____

_____

2. Was the air pressure strong enough to lift several books? _____

_____

3. Write one property of air that allows it to lift objects. _____

_____

4. Can you think of another situation in which air pressure is strong enough to lift a heavy object? _____

_____

_____

_____

Country, Region, or City?

Identify each place as a country, a region, or a city. Then, choose one place to research. Write three facts about the place you chose. Use reference resources if you need help.

1. Egypt _____
2. Dublin _____
3. Costa Rica _____
4. South Pacific _____
5. Oslo _____
6. Canberra _____
7. Belize _____
8. Panama _____
9. Middle East _____
10. Argentina _____
11. Japan_____
12. Great Plains _____
13. Florence_____
14. Pacific Northwest _____
15. Saudi Arabia_____
16. Montreal _____
17. Kenya _____
18. Austria _____
19. Kathmandu _____
20. Arctic Circle _____

_____

_____

_____

BONUS

Geography Terms

Use the geography terms from the word bank to solve the crossword puzzle.

canyon
cape
delta
dune
glacier
isthmus
lagoon
mesa
oasis
pampas
plateau
reservoir
savanna
steppes
strait
tributary

Across

3. roughly triangular land at the mouth of a river formed from deposits of silt
4. semi-dry plains with sparse vegetation
7. Spanish for *table*; steep-sided, flat-topped land
10. water partially or completely enclosed within an atoll
13. water-holding site
14. smaller river or stream that flows into a larger one

Down

1. a narrow piece of land that projects into a body of water
2. narrow strip of land connecting two larger land masses
3. a sandy hill formed by the wind
4. flat, open grassland with scattered trees and shrubs
5. Argentina's flat, grassy plains
6. steep-sided, narrow, deep valley
8. large, slow-moving sheet of ice
9. in a desert, a fertile area with a steady water supply
11. narrow body of water connecting two larger bodies of water
12. large, high, flat area that rises above the surrounding land

North and Central America

Use the letters from the map to identify the following North and Central American countries. Then, choose a country and use reference resources to answer the questions.

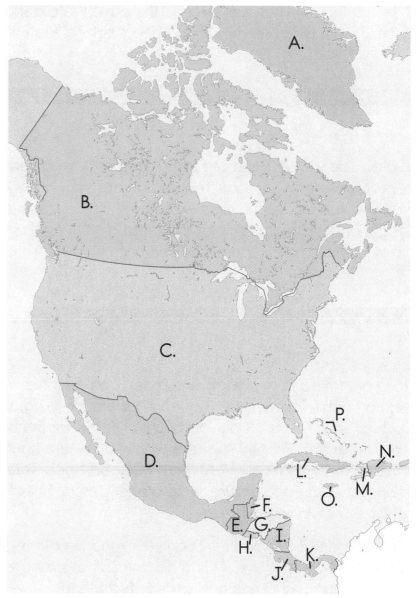

1. _____ El Salvador

2. _____ Greenland

3. _____ Belize

4. _____ United States

5. _____ Nicaragua

6. _____ Canada

7. _____ Mexico

8. _____ Guatemala

9. _____ Honduras

10. _____ Panama

11. _____ Costa Rica

12. _____ Cuba

13. _____ Jamaica

14. _____ Haiti

15. _____ Dominican Republic

16. _____ Bahamas

17. What is the population of the country you chose? _____

18. What form of government does this country have? _____

19. What is the country's capital? _____

BONUS

Take It Outside!

Have a family member join you on a walk around a community park. Bring a pen and a notebook. Record the geographical features you observe in the park, such as streams, rivers, boulders, and hills. Once you return home, make a list of at least 10 prepositions. Then, reflect on your walk around the park. Write a short story or poem about the walk. Incorporate prepositions with the geographical features that you saw.

Go outside with a friend or family member. Take a pencil, a notebook, and a measuring tape. Measure the area in front of and behind where you live. Having someone to help you with the measuring tape will make the task easier. After you have measured the length and width of both places, determine the total area in front of and behind where you live. Which area is larger? How much larger is it?

Take a camera, a notebook, and a pen and go for a walk around your neighborhood with an adult. Take a picture of each landmark or notable place in your neighborhood, such as your home, school, or favorite restaurant. Record each landmark's location in your notebook. Print the pictures when you return home. On a piece of posterboard, create a map that represents your neighborhood. Tape or glue your pictures to the map. Beneath each picture, write a brief description of each landmark or place and why it is shown on your map.

Choose one of the landmarks on your map and write about a memory you have that is associated with it. Use descriptive details that strongly convey a sense of place to your reader. Share your map and story with a friend.

Monthly Goals

Think of three goals to set for yourself this month. For example, you may want to learn five new vocabulary words each week. Write your goals on the lines. Post them someplace visible, where you will see them every day.

Place a check mark next to each goal that you complete. Feel proud that you have met your goals and set new ones to continue to challenge yourself.

1. _____

2. _____

3. _____

Word List

The following words are used in this section. Use a dictionary to look up each word that you do not know. Then, write three sentences. Use at least one word from the word list in each sentence.

abash	interval
census	occupations
demographic	precise
habitat	province
inhabitants	scholars

1. _____

_____

2. _____

_____

3. _____

_____

Introduction to Endurance

This section includes fitness and character development activities that focus on endurance. These activities are designed to get you moving and thinking about developing your physical and mental stamina. If you have limited mobility, feel free to modify any suggested exercises to fit your individual abilities.

Physical Endurance

What do climbing stairs, jogging, and riding your bike have in common? They are all great ways to build endurance! Having endurance means performing an activity for a period of time before your body becomes tired. Improving your endurance requires regular aerobic exercise, which causes your heart to beat faster. You also breathe harder. As a result of regular aerobic activity, your heart becomes stronger, and your blood cells deliver oxygen to your body more efficiently.

Although there are times when a relaxing activity is valuable, it is important to take advantage of the warm mornings and sunny days to go outside. Choose activities that you enjoy. Invite a family member on a walk or a bicycle ride. Play a game of basketball with friends. Leave the relaxing activities for when it is dark, too hot, or raining.

Set an endurance goal this summer. For example, you might jog every day until you can run one mile without stopping. Set new goals when you meet your old ones. Be proud of your endurance success!

Mental Endurance

Showing mental endurance means sticking with something. Staying with a task when you might want to quit and continuing until it is done are ways that you can show mental endurance.

Build your mental endurance this summer. Maybe you want to earn some extra money for a new bike by helping your neighbors with yard work. But, after one week of working in your neighbors' yards, you realize it is not as easy as you thought it would be. Think about some key points, such as how you have wanted that new bike for months. Be positive. Remind yourself that you have only been working for one week and that your neighbors are very appreciative of your work. Think of ways to make the yard work more enjoyable, such as starting earlier in the day or listening to music while you work. Quitting should be the last resort. Build your mental endurance now. It will help prepare you for future challenges.

Solve. Write fractions in simplest form.

1. $15 - (-6) =$ _____

2. $-9 + (-3) =$ _____

3. $-18 + 13 =$ _____

4. $24 + (-16) =$ _____

5. $-32 - (-22) =$ _____

6. $-45 - 30 =$ _____

7. $8\frac{3}{4} + 4\frac{7}{8} =$ _____

8. $5\frac{1}{6} - 2\frac{8}{15} =$ _____

9. $4\frac{5}{7} + 8\frac{1}{2} =$ _____

10. $15\frac{2}{5} - 3\frac{7}{9} =$ _____

11. $5\frac{7}{12} + 13\frac{3}{4} =$ _____

12. $12\frac{9}{11} - 4\frac{1}{2} =$ _____

Draw a line from each dependent clause to the independent clause that completes the sentence.

dependent clause	independent clause
13. If you save your money,	A. Toto got a treat.
14. Because the leaves were changing colors,	B. Jonah's stepfather took him to school.
15. When I see the street sign,	C. I know the movie is good.
16. From the large crowd of people,	D. we knew autumn was here.
17. Since his mother was sick,	E. you can buy a new video game.
18. Because he is a good dog,	F. I know to turn right.
19. but I had to leave early.	G. The game was exciting,

20. Write a dependent clause. _____

_____

21. Now, add an independent clause to the dependent clause to make a complete sentence. _____

_____

DAY 1

Write a definition for each word.

22. firm _____

23. coast _____

24. current _____

Write a definition for each boldfaced word as it is used in the sentence. Then, compare the definitions to your definitions above.

25. My brother works for a law **firm** in Chicago, Illinois. _____
_____

26. Hunter likes to **coast** down that large hill on his bike. _____
_____

27. Zaila let the **current** carry her kayak downstream. _____
_____

Historians study major events from the past, but they also study the lives of everyday people. To do this, historians study the objects and documents that people leave behind. Imagine that you are a historian from the future. What would you learn about 21st-century life from studying your home? Use another sheet of paper if you need more space.

_____

_____

_____

_____

_____

_____

_____

_____

FACTOID: Ninety percent of an iceberg lies beneath the surface of the water.

Rewrite each fraction as a decimal. On the line below each equation, write *T* if the decimal is terminating. Write *R* if the decimal is repeating. Round repeating decimals to the nearest ten thousandth.

1. $\dfrac{7}{8}$ = _____

2. $\dfrac{2}{3}$ = _____

3. $\dfrac{5}{9}$ = _____

4. $\dfrac{5}{6}$ = _____

5. $\dfrac{7}{16}$ = _____

6. $\dfrac{7}{12}$ = _____

Each of the following sentences contains either a compound subject or a compound predicate. Circle the words that make up each compound subject. Underline the words that make up each compound predicate.

7. Corn and green beans are my two favorite vegetables.

8. The game both entertained and excited the football fans.

9. Beth cooked her dinner and then ate it.

10. Diana and I cooked dinner for her parents.

11. Those attending the school picnic sipped lemonade and played games on the

    soccer field.

12. Vanilla and butter pecan are my two favorite flavors of ice cream.

13. Write a sentence about your family that has a compound subject.

    _____

    _____

    _____

14. Write a sentence about a close friend that has a compound predicate.

    _____

    _____

    _____

DAY 2

Paul is getting a new bike. He can get either a racing bike or a mountain bike. His color choices are red, black, and silver. Make a tree diagram showing Paul's possible outcomes. Then, answer the questions. Write fractions in simplest form.

15.   How many possible outcomes are there? _____

16.   What is the probability that Paul will get a racing bike? _____

17.   What is the probability that the bike will be red? _____

18.   What is the probability that Paul will get a silver mountain bike? _____

With which of your family members do you have the most in common? Describe the similarities between you and the person. What do you like to do together? Use another sheet of paper if you need more space.

_____

_____

_____

_____

_____

_____

_____

_____

FITNESS FLASH: Jog in place for 30 seconds.

* See page ii.

If adjectives belong in a specific order (example: *little brown dog*), **no comma between them is needed. However, if you can easily switch the order of adjectives (example:** *energetic, playful dog* or *playful, energetic dog*), **a comma is needed. Read each sentence. If commas are used correctly, make a check mark on the line. If commas are incorrect or missing, make an X on the line.**

1. _____ Elliott was always a nervous anxious cat.

2. _____ The Warrens lived in a gray, ranch house.

3. _____ Saaid wore a green, nylon windbreaker to the game on Friday.

4. _____ Mia and her sister made six jars of fresh, spicy salsa.

5. _____ The friendly eager students waved signs to advertise the car wash.

6. _____ Keely found three blue speckled eggs in the nest.

7. _____ The quaint tiny yellow cottage belongs to Harry's grandma.

8. _____ Linh felt that the thoughtful, encouraging, knowledgeable girl would make a wonderful camp counselor.

Use cross multiplication to solve each proportion.

9. $\dfrac{5}{2} = \dfrac{10}{m}$

10. $\dfrac{3}{a} = \dfrac{9}{3}$

11. $\dfrac{12}{d} = \dfrac{3}{1}$

12. $\dfrac{7}{n} = \dfrac{2}{4}$

13. $\dfrac{p}{15} = \dfrac{6}{5}$

14. $\dfrac{14}{21} = \dfrac{j}{3}$

15. $\dfrac{120}{30} = \dfrac{s}{5}$

16. $\dfrac{y}{18} = \dfrac{3}{6}$

17. $\dfrac{100}{20} = \dfrac{5}{r}$

18. $\dfrac{24}{k} = \dfrac{8}{12}$

19. $\dfrac{g}{15} = \dfrac{8}{5}$

20. $\dfrac{5}{5} = \dfrac{7}{t}$

DAY 3

Read the passage. Then, answer the questions.

Demographics

Demographics are characteristics of human populations. The word *demographics* contains the word roots *demo*, meaning "people," and *graph*, meaning "to write." Demographic data includes people's ages, occupations, educational levels, and incomes. Government officials can use this information to determine the makeup of a city's or county's population and whether there is a need for different services. For example, if a city's officials learn that many families with young children are moving into the area, they may recommend building more schools.

One way that countries collect demographic data is by taking a national census. In the United States, an official census of the population is taken every 10 years. In Canada, a national census is taken every 5 years. Both countries use demographics to examine trends in their populations.

21. What is the main idea of this passage?
    A. Rural cities may have fewer residents than urban ones.
    B. Some cities have a large number of young people.
    C. Demographics include various information about people's lives.

22. What types of information might demographic data include? _____

    _____

23. How do government officials use demographic data? _____

    _____

24. How do countries collect demographic data? _____

    _____

    _____

25. How often are censuses taken in the United States and Canada? _____

    _____

FACTOID: President Lyndon B. Johnson was an elevator operator and a teacher before becoming president.

Calculate unit rates to solve each problem. Round answers as needed.

1. Mikayla can run 2 miles in $12\frac{1}{2}$ minutes. Brie can run 5 miles in $22\frac{1}{4}$ minutes. Who can run faster?

   Unit rate for Mikayla: _____ Unite rate for Brie: _____

   _____ runs faster.

2. Lucy went to Store A and bought $4\frac{4}{5}$ pounds of chicken for $18.50. Sophie went to Store B and bought $3\frac{1}{2}$ pounds of chicken for $14.75. Who got the better deal?

   Unit rate for Lucy's purchase: _____

   Unite rate for Sophie's purchase: _____

   _____ got the better deal.

3. Tré went for a long hike and burned 585 calories in $2\frac{1}{4}$ hours. Zack decided to go for a bike ride and burned 1,055 calories in $3\frac{5}{8}$ hours. Who burned the most calories per hour?

   Unit rate for Tré: _____ Unite rate for Zack: _____

   _____ burned more calories per hour.

Add apostrophes where they are needed in the paragraph.

Family Friends

Camilles best friend is Marcella. Theyre in different classes this year, but theyve known each other since preschool. They havent spent more than a few days apart in their lives. Marcellas mom is Camilles fathers boss. Marcellas father is Camilles uncles business partner. The two families friendship has lasted more than 15 years. Marcella has two older brothers, and Camille has one. Theyre in high school now, but theyll be in college soon. The boys relationship is very close too. They dont hesitate to call one another for advice.

DAY 4

Read each sentence. Then, circle the letter next to the synonym for the boldfaced word. Use a dictionary if you need help.

4. The yearbook includes many **candid** shots of students.
   A. hidden
   B. athletic
   C. difficult
   D. unposed

5. The weather was **balmy** this morning, but it may rain this afternoon.
   A. mild
   B. windy
   C. chilly
   D. stormy

6. The tennis team was **exultant** after its win in the tournament.
   A. upset
   B. bored
   C. angry
   D. thrilled

7. Katie's new dog is **docile** and sweet.
   A. frightened
   B. nervous
   C. calm
   D. energetic

8. Louis's teacher said that Louis is responsible and **competent**.
   A. unhappy
   B. hungry
   C. mischievous
   D. capable

Sprint to Endurance

Interval training is one way to improve your endurance. With interval training, bursts of exercise are followed by short periods of recovery. For this exercise, you will need a pair of comfortable running shoes and a safe, flat place to run and walk.

To begin, jog for several minutes until your muscles are warm. Once you are ready, sprint for 10–15 seconds. Then, walk for 45–60 seconds. Alternate sprinting and walking until you have sprinted five times. Find landmarks, such as mailboxes and trees, to help you time your intervals. For example, you may want to sprint to a mailbox and then walk back, or sprint to a tree and then walk to the next tree before sprinting again.

FITNESS FLASH: Do 10 jumping jacks.

* See page ii.

Solve the multiplication and division problems. If the total number of negative signs is even, the final answer will be positive. If the total number of negative signs is odd, the final answer will be negative. Write fractions in simplest form.

1. $-7 \times 5 =$ _____

2. $32 \div (-4) =$ _____

3. $-9 \times (-3) =$ _____

4. $60 \div (-12) =$ _____

5. $-9 \times 7 =$ _____

6. $-6 \times (-3) =$ _____

7. $4\frac{3}{8} \times 2\frac{1}{3} =$ _____

8. $1\frac{4}{7} \div \frac{1}{2} =$ _____

9. $3\frac{8}{9} \times 1\frac{3}{4} =$ _____

10. $5\frac{2}{3} \div 1\frac{2}{5} =$ _____

11. $4\frac{7}{8} \div 1\frac{1}{4} =$ _____

12. $6\frac{1}{3} \times 2\frac{5}{7} =$ _____

Use the context of each sentence to help you determine the meaning of the underlined word and write it on the line. Then, look up the word in a print or online dictionary to double-check the definition.

13. Dad <u>accelerated</u> once we were on the highway, but he slowed down when he saw the traffic jam ahead.

_____

14. At first it seemed <u>inconceivable</u> that Jordan would be away at camp for two whole weeks, but after a few days, she began to get accustomed to the idea.

_____

15. Mr. Akita apologized for <u>inundating</u> us with homework last week and promised that he would assign a lighter load this week.

_____

16. Sasha was rather <u>aloof</u> at first, but she quickly warmed up to the new kittens and became much friendlier.

_____

17. Maddy described her aunt as a <u>vivacious</u>, enthusiastic woman who loves hiking, dogs, reading mysteries, and painting.

_____

DAY 5

Read each summary. Underline the sentence that does not belong.

18. The topic of the article I read was rain forest plants. Animals like monkeys and sloths live in the rain forest. Numerous flowering plants and vines grow on the forest floor. Many of the trees grow to heights of city buildings. Bromeliads are plants that sometimes grow in the rain forest's canopy.

19. The article, "Today's Computers," describes the many uses of computers. They are used to access the Internet. Word processing programs are used for reports, letters, and schoolwork. They are also used for recreational and educational computer games. Some computers come in different colors.

Read each sentence. Write *M* if the situation describes mechanical weathering. Write *C* if the situation describes chemical weathering.

20. _____ Acid rain dissolves limestone.

21. _____ A large rock falls from a cliff and breaks.

22. _____ Water in the cracks of a rock freezes and breaks apart the rock.

23. _____ An old car sitting outside for several years forms rust on its underside.

24. _____ Tree roots crack the foundation of a house.

25. _____ Moss grows on the surface of a rock, producing pits.

26. _____ The edges of a rock become rounded over time as water carries it along the bottom of a stream.

27. _____ A marble gravestone in an area with high pollutants becomes difficult to read over time.

28. _____ Wind blows sand against a rock formation in the desert.

> **CHARACTER CHECK:** Write a story about a character who demonstrates diligence.

Write and solve an equation for each problem.

1. Charley sold 12 fruit baskets for the school fundraiser. Maria sold 15, and Paul sold 18. If each fruit basket cost $18, how much money did they raise altogether?

   equation: _____

   answer: _____

2. A cougar can run 25 miles per hour. A cheetah can run 55 miles per hour. If they both run for 3 hours at full speed, how much farther will the cheetah run?

   equation: _____

   answer: _____

3. Elsa sold 24 drawings for $12 each at the art fair. She is going to use $\frac{1}{3}$ of the money to buy books. The rest of the money is going into her savings account. How much money will she put into her savings account?

   equation: _____

   answer: _____

4. Lukas paid for a pair of shoes with a $50 bill. After the clerk added 9% tax to the purchase, Lukas received $17.30 in change. What was the price of the shoes, not including the tax?

   equation: _____

   answer: _____

Write commas where they are needed in the paragraph.

Jarvis and Rover

Jarvis is a kind helpful honest friend. He has short black hair and large brown friendly eyes. When I go to Jarvis's house, we play with his dog Rover. Rover is a gentle quiet dog. His tail is long thin and feathery. His ears are floppy soft and silky. They fly behind him when he runs. Rover is always ready to plant a big sloppy kiss on my cheek. Just like Jarvis Rover likes everybody and everybody likes him.

Read the passage. Then, answer the questions.

The Vikings in Canada

The Vikings were the first Europeans to cross the Atlantic Ocean and reach North America. Historians knew that the Vikings settled in Greenland and Iceland but were not sure how much time they spent in Canada. In 1960, a Viking settlement from around AD 1000 was found at L'Anse aux Meadows in what is now the Canadian province of Newfoundland and Labrador. Archaeologists uncovered the ruins of eight buildings that had sod walls and roofs over supporting frames. In the middle of each floor was a long, narrow fireplace used for heating and cooking. Archaeologists also found tools the Vikings had used. Because the design of the tools and the buildings was similar to those found in Viking settlements in Greenland and Iceland, it was clear that the Vikings settled in Canada as well. Today, L'Anse aux Meadows is a national historic site, and many people visit it each year.

5. What is the main idea of this passage?

  A. Archaeologists uncovered the ruins of eight buildings.

  B. The first Europeans to reach North America were the Vikings.

  C. Many people visit national historic sites each year.

6. In which area of Canada did the Vikings settle?

  _____

7. What was found in 1960 at L'Anse aux Meadows ?

  _____

8. What did the buildings at L'Anse aux Meadows look like?

  _____

  _____

9. How did archaeologists know that it was a Viking settlement?

  _____

  _____

FACTOID: Two stars that orbit each other are called *doubles* or *binary stars*. Half of the stars in the universe are doubles.

Write equivalent expressions.

1. $6x + 7 - 3 + x =$ _____

2. $4(3y + 5) =$ _____

3. $-2w + w - (3 + 7) =$ _____

4. $2b(b - 2) =$ _____

5. $-9(3x + 7) =$ _____

6. $c + c + 2c - 12 =$ _____

7. $a \times 5 \times a =$ _____

8. $12 \div (z - 3) =$ _____

9. $6 \times 2d \times 3 =$ _____

10. $x + 5x - 3x + 6 =$ _____

Write quotation marks where they are needed in each sentence.

11. Morgan shouted, Hurray! We made it!

12. Have you been a part of a sports team at your school? asked Silvia.

13. After you take out the trash, said my dad, we can go see a movie.

14. Reid told Angie that Casey at the Bat was his favorite poem.

15. Look out for that bump in the road! shouted Dad.

16. Leave your binoculars at home, suggested Ms. Haynes. Your ears will be more helpful than your eyes on this field trip.

17. What is the quickest way to get to the park? asked Andre.

18. We are going to the movies this afternoon, said Deanna, and then we are going to get ice cream.

19. Be careful! shouted Mom.

DAY 7

Read the words in the word bank. Complete the outline by writing the subheadings and supporting details on the lines. Use each word or phrase once.

books	chairs	desks
furniture	library books	paper
pencils	pens	reference books
storage cabinets	supplies	textbooks

Classroom

A. _____

    1. _____

    2. _____

    3. _____

B. _____

    1. _____

    2. _____

    3. _____

C. _____

    1. _____

    2. _____

    3. _____

A *primary source* provides information about an event from someone who was present when the event occurred. A *secondary source* collects and interprets information from other sources after an event has happened. Read each description. Write *P* if the source is a primary source. Write *S* if the source is a secondary source.

20. _____ a diary

21. _____ an encyclopedia

22. _____ a textbook

23. _____ a photograph

24. _____ a biography

25. _____ a history book

26. _____ a letter

27. _____ a birth certificate

28. _____ an interview

29. _____ taped news footage

FITNESS FLASH: Hop on your left foot 10 times.

* See page ii.

Write and solve an addition equation for each problem. It may be useful to include absolute values in the equations you write.

1. The Trailride Bus left Pottstown and drove 54 miles due east. Then, it turned around and drove due west for 73 miles. How far was the bus from Pottstown?

   Addition equation: _____

2. The temperature was 32° at dawn. By noon, the temperature had risen 15°. By midnight, the temperature had fallen again by 57°. What was the temperature at midnight?

   Addition equation: _____

3. Delaney rolled a 6 and moved his game piece forward 6 spaces on the board. Then, he drew a card that read *Move back 10 spaces*. How many spaces is he from where he began his turn?

   Addition equation: _____

Write quotation marks where they are needed in the paragraph.

Our Special Spring Program

Holly Street Middle School will hold a spring program next month. I will be the

announcer for the program. I will say, The drama team is proud to present a famous

story about a young woman who was too curious. After the drama team's performance,

Mr. Graham's class will recite The Cloud by Percy Bysshe Shelley. Ms. Carrol's class will

sing The Ashe Grove.

DAY 8

Read each situation. Then, answer the question to predict what will happen next.

Sally Ann is 80 years old. She lives in a house with a small, fenced yard. She decided to adopt a dog to keep her company. Sally Ann went to the animal shelter and narrowed her choice to two dogs. The first was a large, one-year-old retriever. He had a lot of energy and was accustomed to running on acres of land. The second dog was a small, three-year-old spaniel. He was very calm and knew how to use a doggy door to go out into the yard.

4. Which dog do you think Sally Ann will choose? Why?_____

_____

_____

Harry's weekend was busy. He spent Friday night at Roberto's house, and they stayed up late watching movies. Harry left early the next morning for baseball practice. He was exhausted when he finally returned home, but he helped his mom get ready for the party they were hosting that evening. When all of the preparations were finished, Harry went to his room and eyed his bed. He still had three hours before the party began.

5. What do you think will happen next? Why? _____

_____

_____

Pretend that people on Earth have finally learned how to live on other planets. Which planet would you most like to live on other than Earth? Why did you choose that planet? You can use some research materials to help you decide your answer. Use another sheet of paper if you need more space.

_____

_____

_____

_____

FACTOID: The sun's diameter is approximately 870,000 miles (1,400,000 km).

A unit rate can also be called the *constant of proportionality* (*k*). It describes the rate at which variables in an equation change. It is found using the equation
k = *x* ÷ *y*. Find the constant of proportionality for the set of values below. Then, complete the table with three more values. Graph the points on the coordinate plane and draw a line through the points to show that the rate of change is constant (a straight line).

x	3	6	_____	_____	_____
y	1	2	_____	_____	_____

k = _____

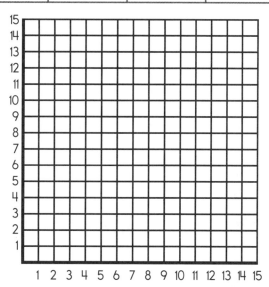

Write a sentence using each word. Beside the word, write *positive*, *neutral*, or *negative* to show the connotation of the word as you used it.

1. unique _____

   _____

2. flimsy _____

   _____

3. rustic _____

   _____

4. immature _____

   _____

Read the poem. Then, answer the questions.

Emily Dickinson

During her lifetime, Emily Dickinson published only 7 of the approximately 1,800 poems that she wrote. Most of her poems were published posthumously, or after her death. Today, Dickinson is known for her unusual use of capital letters and punctuation, vivid imagery, slant rhyme, and broken meter. She did not give her poems titles. Instead, Dickinson's poems are often organized in chronological order and assigned a number based on when scholars think each poem was written.

254

"Hope" is the thing with feathers –
That perches in the soul –
And sings the tune without the words –
And never stops – at all –

And sweetest – in the Gale – is heard –
And sore must be the storm –
That could abash the little Bird –
That kept so many warm –

I've heard it in the chilliest land –
And on the strangest Sea –
Yet, never, in Extremity,
It asked a crumb – of Me.

5. To what does Emily Dickinson compare hope? _____

6. What do you think Dickinson means when she writes that hope is ". . . sweetest – in the Gale. . ."? _____

    _____

7. When words sound the same but do not rhyme exactly, they are called *slant rhymes*. Write one pair of slant rhymes from the poem.

    _____ / _____

 FITNESS FLASH: Hop on your right foot for 30 seconds.

* See page ii.

Find the circumference of each circle using the formula C=2πr. The variable *r* stands for *radius.* Use 3.14 for pi (π).

1.
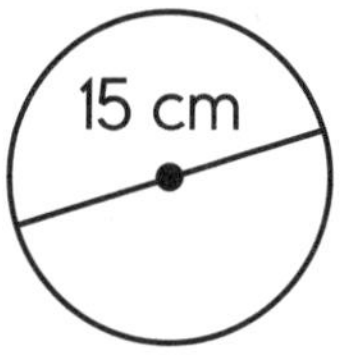

____

2.
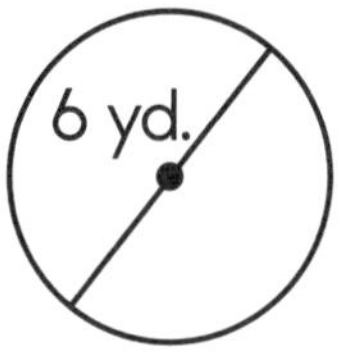

____

3.
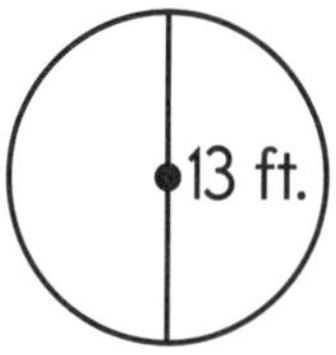

____

4.
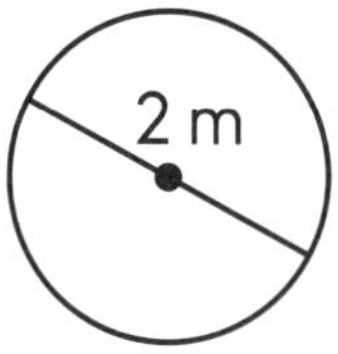

____

5.
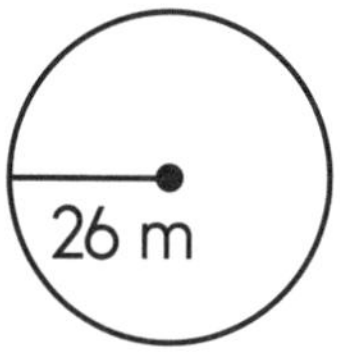

____

6.

____

7.

____

8.

____

Write hyphens where they are needed in each sentence.

9. The sports loving fans did not seem to notice the freezing temperatures.
10. Ilene made her mother in law a chocolate cake for her birthday.
11. The store has forty four electric fans in stock.
12. Mikacia saw twenty one meteors in the pitch black sky.
13. Fifty eight people waited two hours in the late afternoon drizzle for tickets to see the movie.

Write two sentences. Use at least one hyphen in each sentence.

14. ____

15. ____

DAY 10

Read each paragraph. Circle the accessory that each paragraph describes. Then, underline the context clues that helped you choose your answer.

16. Sharon was looking for something to carry on her business trip. She wanted it to be large enough to hold her money, glasses, and address book. She preferred that it would have a shoulder strap and match the clothes she was taking.

A. wallet   B. purse
C. suitcase   D. backpack

17. Sharon stopped at a store. She told the salesperson where she was going and what clothes she was taking. She explained that the most important thing was that she be comfortable while standing all day and demonstrating her product. Sharon sat down to try on some of the things the salesperson brought her.

A. hat   B. shoes
C. luggage   D. belt

Label the diagram of Earth's interior using the terms from the word bank. Use reference resources if you need help.

| asthenosphere | inner core | mantle |
| crust | lithosphere | outer core |

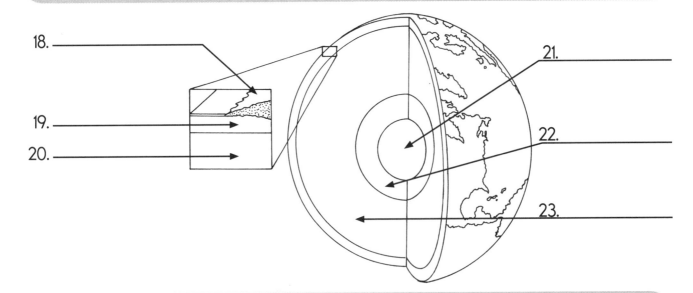

18. _____

19. _____

20. _____

21. _____

22. _____

23. _____

CHARACTER CHECK: Make a list of five ways that you can show integrity.

Find the area of each circle using the formula $A = \pi r^2$. Use 3.14 for pi (π). Round answers to the nearest whole number.

1.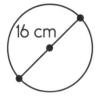
16 cm

_____

2.
18 km

_____

3.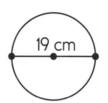
19 cm

_____

4.
8 ft.

_____

5.
22 cm

_____

6.
5 m

_____

7.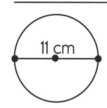
11 cm

_____

8.
14 in.

_____

Follow the instructions to write comparisons.

9. Write a metaphor related to weather.

_____

10. Write a simile that includes something related to the beach.

_____

11. Write a sentence personifying something musical.

_____

12. Write a metaphor that includes a sound or a noise.

_____

13. Write a sentence personifying an animal.

_____

14. Write a metaphor about a season.

_____

15. Write a sentence personifying a piece of furniture.

_____

DAY 11

Circle the letter next to the word that completes each analogy.

16. Chapter : book :: act : _____.

   A. novel   B. comedy   C. play   D. sitcom

17. Thrifty : miserly :: smart : _____.

   A. cheap   B. foolish   C. gullible   D. brilliant

18. Waltz : dance :: oak : _____.

   A. acorn   B. tree   C. pine   D. tango

19. Reveal : divulge :: hide : _____.

   A. discover   B. imagine   C. conceal   D. inform

20. Stiff : flexible :: empty : _____.

   A. low   B. rigid   C. full   D. elastic

A *fault* is a break in Earth's crust where pieces of the crust slip past each other. There are three main kinds of faults: *normal*, *reverse*, and *strike-slip*. Label each diagram by writing the type of fault it represents. Use reference resources if you need help.

21. This type of fault is caused by tension forces.

_____

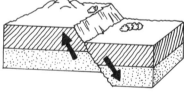

22. This type of fault is caused by shear forces.

_____

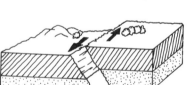

23. This type of fault is caused by compression forces.

_____

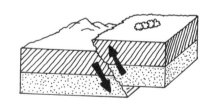

FACTOID: The world's oldest known living tree, a conifer in Sweden, has a root system that has been growing for more than 9,500 years.

Increase each rectangle by a scale factor of 2. Then, find the area and perimeter using the new measurements.

1.
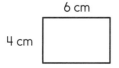
6 cm
4 cm

A = _____ P = _____

2.

12 in.

A = _____ P = _____

3.
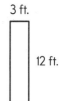
3 ft.
12 ft.

A = _____ P = _____

4.
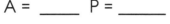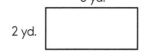
8 yd.
2 yd.

A = _____ P = _____

5.
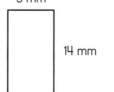
5 mm
14 mm

A = _____ P = _____

6.
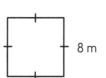
8 m

A = _____ P = _____

Look up each word in an online or print dictionary. Circle the syllable that is stressed. Then, write the word's part of speech and definition on the line. If it has more than one definition and part of speech, use the first one listed.

7. benevolent _____

_____

8. correlate _____

_____

9. synopsis _____

_____

10. indisputably _____

_____

11. psoriasis _____

_____

12. abrasion _____

_____

13. amiable _____

_____

Read the passage. Then, answer the questions.

Giant Superstars

In December 2000, two giant pandas arrived in the United States from China. The pair was delivered to the National Zoo in Washington, D.C. Their names are Mei Xiang (may SHONG) and Tian Tian (t-YEN t-YEN). In July 2005, Mei Xiang and Tian Tian had a cub. When he was 100 days old, he was given the name Tai Shan (tie SHON), which means "peaceful mountain." Eight years later, the couple added to the family again. A female cub named Bao Bao, or "treasure," was born in August of 2013.

The pandas' exhibit has both indoor and outdoor areas where they can roam freely. Because pandas dislike hot, humid weather, the outdoor habitat is air-conditioned. Visitors can watch the pandas graze on bamboo shoots, apples, carrots, and special biscuits.

Giant pandas are rare and have always been popular in zoos. Only about 1,600 remain in the wild. They live in the mountain forests in China. Pandas face dangers from poachers and the destruction of their habitats. The Chinese government has made a tradition of loaning or giving pandas to other countries as a symbol of friendship. This new pair of pandas is on loan to the United States. The United States must pay a $1 million per year "rental fee" for Mei Xiang and Tian Tian.

14. Why do you think giant pandas are among the most popular attractions at zoos throughout the world? _____

15. Describe the pandas' exhibit at the National Zoo. _____

_____

_____

16. Why does the Chinese government loan or give pandas to other countries?

_____

_____

17. How does the author organize information in the passage? Is the transition from information about specific pandas to pandas in general effective? Explain.

_____

_____

_____

Find the missing edge length.

1. $V = 375$ m³

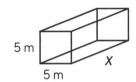

5 m
5 m
x

x = _____

2. $V = 1,056$ m³

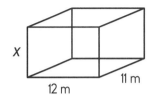

x
12 m
11 m

x = _____

3. $V = 2,340$ cm³

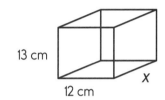

13 cm
12 cm
x

x = _____

4. $V = 280$ ft.³

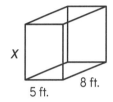

x
5 ft.
8 ft.

x = _____

Write semicolons and commas where they are needed in each sentence.

5. Marcy forgot to bring a suitcase Mindy remembered.

6. So far this month, John has traveled to Jackson Mississippi Tallahassee Florida and Nashville Tennessee.

7. Casey looked forward to the weekend his uncle was coming to visit.

8. Jonah's class made lunch for Mr. Burns the custodian Mrs. Fry the head cook and Miss Bookman the librarian.

9. Sometimes we stay late after practice however we leave when the coach goes home.

FITNESS FLASH: Do 10 jumping jacks.

* See page ii.

Circle the letter next to the word that completes each analogy.

10. Sour : lemon :: sweet : _____.

 A. cake B. water C. flowers D. rice

11. Vine : grapes :: tree : _____.

 A. bird B. nuts C. lumber D. swing

12. Sip : beverage :: chew : _____.

 A. food B. water C. dirt D. fork

13. Vegetable : corn :: candy : _____.

 A. yellow B. wrapper C. eat D. peppermint

14. Song : songwriter :: book : _____.

 A. author B. person C. singer D. agent

Perseverance Interview

Perseverance means not giving up, even if something is difficult to do. Talk with family members about perseverance. Encourage them to tell you about people they know who demonstrate the quality of perseverance.

Select one person that your family mentioned. Contact this person, and ask if you can conduct an interview. Ask specific questions to help you understand the challenges the person overcame to be successful. After the interview, choose one of the options below as a way of sharing your appreciation to the person you interviewed.

 A. Write the person a note highlighting what you learned and how the person's story of persevering affected you personally.

 B. Make a poster that highlights the person's accomplishments. Include an appropriate slogan that you will be able to use in your own life.

FACTOID: The Pacific barreleye fish has a transparent head.

Given the volume, find the edge length of each cube.

1.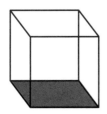

V = 125 cm³

side = _____

2.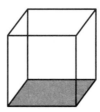

V = 8 ft.³

side = _____

3.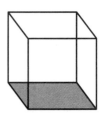

V = 343 yd.³

side = _____

4.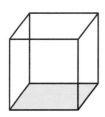

V = 1,000 mm³

side = _____

5.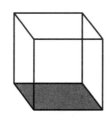

V = 1,728 in.³

side = _____

6.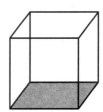

V = 1 m³

side = _____

Write colons where they are needed in each phrase or sentence.

7. At 3 00 P.M., everyone in class needs to take the following items to the auditorium a pencil, an eraser, and a notebook.

8. To Whom It May Concern

9. I need a few things to make a new recipe corn, tomatoes, onions, black beans, and cilantro.

Write a sentence that includes a direct quotation. The sentence has been started for you. Remember to add a colon where it is needed.

One of my favorite songs begins with _____

_____

_____

_____

DAY 14

Jayla, Judy, Chuck, and Bill have different jobs: lifeguard, lawyer, pilot, and professor. Each drives a different type of vehicle: truck, motorcycle, bike, or car. Use the chart and the clues to determine each person's job and vehicle.

- Jayla is afraid of flying.
- Judy gets to her office on a vehicle that has two wheels.
- For Chuck's job, he often passes through two or three states each day.
- The person who is the lifeguard also drives the truck.
- A man rides a bike to his job.
- A man needs a large trunk to bring graded papers back and forth to work.

	Lifeguard	Lawyer	Pilot	Professor
Jayla				
Judy				
Chuck				
Bill				

Imagine that a family from another country is visiting your town or city. What should they see? Where should they go? Create a five-day itinerary for the family that explores your town's or city's landmarks and attractions. Use another sheet of paper if you need more space.

_____

_____

_____

_____

_____

 FITNESS FLASH: Jog in place for 30 seconds.

* See page ii.

Solve for each variable.

1. $\dfrac{5}{6} = \dfrac{n}{36}$

2. $\dfrac{3}{8} = \dfrac{x}{24}$

3. $\dfrac{5}{7} = \dfrac{b}{42}$

4. $\dfrac{8}{9} = \dfrac{p}{63}$

$n =$ _____

$x =$ _____

$b =$ _____

$p =$ _____

Use equal ratios to solve each problem.

5. The Dollar-Mart grocery store sells 6 bars of soap for $1.00. How many bars of soap can a customer buy with $9.00?

6. Kelsey's soccer team scored 5 points in 2 games. At this rate, how many points will the team score in 16 games?

7. The O'Neil family is driving 60 miles per hour. If they continue to drive at this speed, how many miles will they drive in 4 hours?

Write the abbreviation for each word. Add periods when needed.

8. Mister _____

9. ounce _____

10. yard _____

11. Company _____

12. Captain _____

13. inch _____

14. Association _____

15. Avenue _____

16. et cetera _____

17. Doctor _____

18. Missus _____

19. feet _____

20. Street _____

21. pound _____

22. Junior _____

23. Incorporated _____

24. Senior _____

25. Boulevard _____

26. United States _____

27. General _____

28. Professor _____

DAY 15

Read the passage. Then, answer the questions.

Matthew Henson

The man stood in the cold, white world, waiting for the other sleds to arrive. Suddenly, he realized that he was standing farther north than any other person in history.

The explorer was an African American man named Matthew Henson. He was on an expedition with Robert Peary to the North Pole, but it was not the first time Henson had made this journey. He had worked for Peary for more than 20 years. He had been with Peary all of the times the explorer had tried to make it to the North Pole and failed. In 1908, Peary decided to try one last time. He insisted that Henson go with him.

Matthew Henson was of great help to Peary. He knew how to survive in the Arctic. He became friends with the native inhabitants and learned their language. He used their information to help him plan the final expedition. Henson's plans with Peary were precise. The team put **caches**, or stockpiles, of food in igloos along the trail. They would use this food on their way back after they ran out of supplies from the sleds. Henson was the best driver of the dog teams, so he took the lead and broke the trail. This time, the team was successful. On April 6, 1909, Matthew Henson stood with Peary and their crew at the northernmost place on Earth.

29. What does the word *caches* mean in the passage? _____

30. Number the events in the order they happened.

    _____ Robert Peary says that he will make one more trip to the Arctic.

    _____ Matthew Henson starts working for Robert Peary.

    _____ Matthew Henson carefully plans the final trip to the North Pole.

    _____ Matthew Henson stands at the North Pole for the first time.

31. When did Henson reach the northernmost place on Earth?_____

    _____

32. What role did the native inhabitants of the area play in Peary's and Henson's

    successful expedition? _____

    _____

> **CHARACTER CHECK: In the evening, discuss with an adult how you demonstrated honesty today.**

Draw each polygon according to the given conditions.

1. a quadrilateral with 1 pair of parallel sides and 2 congruent sides	2. a regular polygon with 6 congruent sides
3. a polygon with 1 right angle and 2 acute angles	4. a quadrilateral with 2 pairs of parallel sides and 4 congruent sides

Identify each sentence as simple (S), compound (C), complex (CX), or compound-complex (CCX).

5. _____ Amelia planned to do her report on Georgia O'Keeffe, but she ended up switching her topic to Frida Kahlo.

6. _____ Have you visited Mount Rushmore in South Dakota?

7. _____ Although Talesha had overdue fines at the library, she was still able to check out her books, and she planned to return the next day to pay the fines.

8. _____ Sam and Neil helped the girls decorate the gym for the dance.

9. _____ Not only are cockroaches household pests, studies show that the majority of these insects carry bacteria that can cause food poisoning.

10. _____ Are you ordering seafood tonight, or are you planning to choose a vegetarian dish?

11. _____ Despite the severe storm warning, the concert has not been canceled.

12. _____ The anaconda is a type of South American water snake.

DAY 16

Write and solve an equation for each problem.

13. Nola is going with her class on an overnight field trip. The cost of the trip is $45 per student. The price includes $21 to cover the cost of the hotel. Nola will also receive three meal tickets. Each meal ticket costs the same amount. How much does each meal ticket cost?

   equation: _____

   cost of each meal ticket: _____

14. Melinda sells drinks at a football game. First, she pays a vendor $30 for a tray of 24 sodas. Then, she sells the sodas in the stands. She makes $42 profit for each tray of sodas she sells. How much does Melinda charge for each soda?

   equation: _____

   cost of each soda: _____

Write the letter of each term next to its definition.

15. _____ water in the form of rain, snow, sleet, or hail falls from clouds onto Earth's surface

16. _____ the process by which clouds form as water vapor cools and changes into liquid water droplets

17. _____ how water soaks into the ground

18. _____ water that flows across land and into streams, rivers, or oceans

19. _____ the process by which water on Earth's surface changes from liquid to water vapor

20. _____ evaporation of water into the atmosphere from the leaves and stems of plants

A. condensation

B. evaporation

C. infiltration

D. precipitation

E. runoff

F. transpiration

FACTOID: The average summer temperature in Antarctica is 35.6°F (2°C).

Find the measure of the missing angle in each triangle. Then, classify the triangle as *acute*, *right*, **or** *obtuse*.

1.
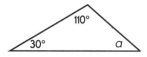

a = _____

_____

2.
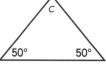

c = _____

_____

3.
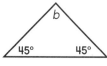

b = _____

_____

4.
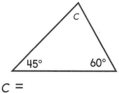

c = _____

_____

5.
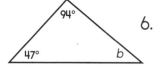

b = _____

_____

6.
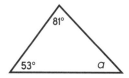

a = _____

_____

7.
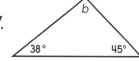

b = _____

_____

8.

a = _____

_____

Write the letter of each sentence next to the sentence that explains its meaning.

9. A. Stop that girl Meg.
    B. Stop that girl, Meg.

_____ You are asking someone to stop a girl named Meg.
_____ You are asking Meg to stop a girl.

10. A. I will ask, Jade.
    B. I will ask Jade.

_____ You are telling Jade you will ask someone a question.
_____ You will ask Jade a question.

11. A. Help them push Kendall.
    B. Help them push, Kendall.

_____ You are asking Kendall to help others push something.
_____ You are asking someone to help push Kendall, possibly on a sled or swing.

12. A. Call her Rebecca.
    B. Call her, Rebecca.

_____ You are telling Rebecca to call another girl.
_____ You are telling someone to call a girl by the name Rebecca.

DAY 17

Circle the letter next to the answer for each question about using a dictionary.

13. The guide words are *justice* and *juvenile*. Locate the word *just*.

    A.   previous page   B.   this page   C.   next page

14. The guide words are *wonder* and *woodsy*. Which word is not on the page?

    A.   wood   B.   won   C.   woodchuck

15. Look at the guide words. On which page will you find the word *frugal*?

    A.   froth–fruit   B.   fuji–funny   C.   full–fumble

16. The guide words are *yearbook* and *yellow jacket*. Which word is on the page?

    A.   yellow   B.   year   C.   yelp

17. Which word will be last on the page?

    A.   payable   B.   payee   C.   pay

18. Which word will be first on the page?

    A.   halfpenny   B.   half   C.   halfway

19. The guide words are *sealant* and *seatrain*. Which word is not on the page?

    A.   seat   B.   seem   C.   search

20. The guide words are *applesauce* and *apply*. Which word is on the page?

    A.   appreciate   B.   application   C.   apple

High-Knees Drill

Have you ever wondered how a football player gains the speed and agility to run through players and score? He regularly does the high-knees drill! Begin by placing five soft objects in a row, approximately five feet apart. Then, with knees high and eyes straight ahead, run full speed over each object. For an added challenge, try holding a ball while running. Set monthly goals to increase the number of times that you do this drill, and watch as your speed and endurance improve.

FITNESS FLASH: Hop on your right foot for 30 seconds.

* See page ii.

Use the diagram to answer each question.

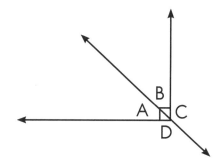

1. m∠A + m∠B = _____

    These are called _____ angles.

2. m∠D + m∠ _____ = 180°

    These are called _____ angles.

Use the diagram to answer each question.

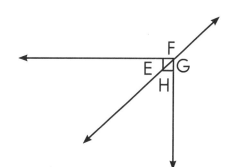

3. If m∠H = 43°,

    m∠E = _____

    m∠G = _____

    m∠F = _____

4. If m∠G = 132°,

    m∠H = _____

    m∠E = _____

    m∠F = _____

Follow the directions to write sentences.

5. Write a simple sentence. _____

    _____

6. Write a complex sentence. _____

    _____

7. Write a compound sentence. _____

    _____

8. Write a compound-complex sentence. _____

    _____

DAY 18

Read the passage. Then, answer the questions.

from *Black Beauty* by Anna Sewell

While I was young I lived upon my mother's milk, as I could not eat grass. In the daytime I ran by her side, and at night I lay down close by her. When it was hot we used to stand by the pond in the shade of the trees, and when it was cold we had a nice warm shed near the grove.

As soon as I was old enough to eat grass my mother used to go out to work in the daytime, and come back in the evening.

There were six young colts in the meadow besides me; they were older than I was; some were nearly as large as grown-up horses. I used to run with them, and had great fun; we used to gallop all together round and round the field as hard as we could go. Sometimes we had rather rough play, for they would frequently bite and kick as well as gallop.

One day, when there was a good deal of kicking, my mother whinnied to me to come to her, and then she said:

"I wish you to pay attention to what I am going to say to you. The colts who live here are very good colts, but they are cart-horse colts, and of course they have not learned manners. You have been well-bred and well-born; your father has a great name in these parts, and your grandfather won the cup two years at the Newmarket races; your grandmother had the sweetest temper of any horse I ever knew, and I think you have never seen me kick or bite. I hope you will grow up gentle and good, and never learn bad ways; do your work with a good will, lift your feet up well when you trot, and never bite or kick even in play."

9. From whose point of view is this passage told? How does using this point of view contribute to the story? _____

10. What is the setting for this selection? _____

11. According to his mother, how is Black Beauty different from the other colts he plays with? _____

12. Go to the library and borrow an audio version of *Black Beauty*. Or, look for a movie version. Listen to the story or view the film. How is your experience different from reading a passage from the book? On a separate sheet of paper, compare and contrast your experiences.

Look at the 3 x 3 arrangements of dots below. How many squares can be made from 9 dots if you use the dots to mark their corners? Use the grids below to show all of the squares that you can make. Hint: There are more than 5 squares.

Add or remove punctuation where it is needed in the paragraph.

School Newspaper Survey

Our school newspaper (*The Bobcat Times* took a survey last week The results were published today. The first survey question was What's your favorite movie. Two fifths of the students preferred big surprise—*March of the Penguins*. The girls favorite film was *The Incredibles* the boys favorite was *Harry Potter and the Chamber of Secrets*. The second survey question was What's your favorite poem?" The sixth grade students' favorites were the following Toothpaste by Michael Rosen "The Honey Pot" by Alan Riddell and Mean Song" by Eve Merriam.

DAY 19

Write the best resource to use for each task.

1. locate the pronunciation of *scrivener* _____

2. find a different word for *excellent* _____

3. determine the continent(s) that border(s) Asia _____

4. find more than 15 definitions for *run* _____

5. find the definition of *scalene* in your math book _____

6. locate the pages in your science book that refer to plant roots _____

7. gather information about castles for your class report _____

8. find the definition of *genealogy* in your social studies book _____

9. label the countries of South America on a map_____

10. find seven facts about roller coasters _____

If you could add a holiday to the calendar that everyone in the country would celebrate, what would it be, when would it be, and how would it be celebrated? Use a separate piece of paper if you need more space.

_____

_____

_____

_____

_____

_____

_____

 FITNESS FLASH: Hop on your left foot 10 times.

* See page ii.

Solve each problem. Draw and label your answers in the space provided.

1. Phoebe has 9 rocks. She puts the rocks into 3 boxes. Each box has 1 more rock than the previous box. How many rocks are in each box?

2. Alyssa has 4 boxes that contain a total of 30 seeds. Three of the boxes contain the same number of seeds. The fourth box contains the sum of the other 3 boxes. How many seeds are in each box?

Use a print or online thesaurus to find a synonym for each word below.

3. originate _____

4. preposterous _____

5. sustenance _____

6. mandate _____

7. obtrusive _____

8. rebuke _____

9. sinister _____

10. contemplate _____

11. deviate _____

12. enigma_____

DAY 20

Circle the letter next to the best resource to use for each task.

13. In which reference book would you find the best map of your country?

    A. dictionary   B. atlas   C. thesaurus

14. In which reference book would you find the definition of the word *congregate*?

    A. dictionary   B. atlas   C. encyclopedia

15. In which reference book would you find information about the history and economy of Honduras?

    A. dictionary   B. thesaurus   C. encyclopedia

16. In which reference book would you find what time the sun will rise tomorrow?

    A. dictionary   B. almanac   C. atlas

Write the word from the word bank that matches each description.

demand	profit	inflation	scarcity	supply

17. the amount of a good or service that people are willing and able to purchase at a given price _____

18. an increase in the average cost of goods and services _____

19. the amount of a product available for sale _____

20. when there are not enough goods and services available to meet demand

    _____

21. The amount of money that a company makes after paying for all supplies, resources, and overhead costs _____

> **CHARACTER CHECK:** Do something thoughtful for a friend or family member today, such as helping fold laundry or taking out the trash.

The Doppler Effect

Why does the sound of a buzzer change as the buzzer moves closer or farther away?

Have you noticed that the sound of a car as it approaches is different from its sound after it passes? This is because the sound waves produced by the car have a higher frequency as the car approaches you and a lower frequency as the car travels away from you. This is called the Doppler effect. In this activity, you will demonstrate the Doppler effect.

Materials:
- small buzzer
- audio recorder
- plastic tub of water
- pebble

Procedure:
Hold the buzzer in front of the audio recorder. Turn on the buzzer and record the sound. Play the recording to make sure that it sounds the same as the buzzer's original sound.

Record the buzzer's sound again. This time, move the buzzer toward and away from the recorder several times. Play the recording and listen to how the buzzer's pitch (the highness or lowness of a sound) changes during the recording.

1. Describe the difference between the first recording and the second recording.

_____

_____

Drop the pebble into the plastic tub of water. Watch the ripples in the water. These ripples show what happens when something makes a sound and the air vibrates. The sound waves spread in every direction, similar to the water ripples. These ripples look like the sound waves that the buzzer made when you held it still in front of the recorder.

Drag your fingers across the water's surface. These ripples look like the sound waves when you moved the buzzer toward and away from the recorder. The sound waves near the buzzer are closer, which makes the sound's pitch higher. When the buzzer is farther from the recorder, the sound waves are farther apart and the pitch is lower.

2. Describe how the ripples created by dropping the pebble into the water are different from the ripples created by dragging your fingers across the water.

_____

_____

BONUS

Solar "Still" Works

What is a solar still? How does a solar still work?

Solar energy is a renewable resource because, unlike energy resources such as oil and coal, it is quickly replenished. Renewable energy can help solve environmental problems, such as drought. In some coastal areas where there are low levels of freshwater for drinking and farming, people use a device called a solar still to create freshwater. In this activity, you will create a solar still and discover how it works.

Materials:
- clear glass measuring cup
- teaspoon
- large plastic cup
- plastic wrap
- small rock
- water
- salt
- small paper cup
- rubber band

Procedure:
Fill the measuring cup with 8 ounces (0.24 L) of water and 1–2 teaspoons (4.9–9.8 mL) of salt. Stir the water and salt until the salt dissolves. Dip your finger in the water and taste it.

Pour about 2 ounces (1/4 cup) of salt water into the large plastic cup. Place the small paper cup inside the large cup so that it floats. Then, cover the large cup with plastic wrap, and secure it tightly with the rubber band. Place the small rock in the middle of the plastic wrap so that it sags slightly. Do not allow the rock to touch the salt water or rip the plastic wrap.

Place the cups in a sunny location, and check them after a few hours. Record your observations on the lines. After a few days, check the cups by removing the plastic wrap. Record your observations. Dip your finger into the small cup's water and taste it.

Observations:

1. How was solar energy used in this activity? _____

_____

_____

2. How might this method be used on a larger scale?_____

_____

_____

Straight to the Source!

What primary sources do you create each day?

A primary source provides information about an event from someone who was present when that event occurred. Letters, photographs, diaries, artifacts, and news footage are examples of primary sources. You probably create several primary sources every day, sometimes without even realizing it!

1. List five activities you participated in during the last 24 hours. Beside each activity, write any evidence, such as cash register receipts, that you left behind.

    _____

    _____

    _____

    _____

    _____

2. List any personal records that you created, such as text messages, a social media post, or a photograph. _____

    _____

    _____

3. Would your activities be mentioned in a primary source, such as a friend's journal entry, a government record, or the local newspaper? If so, list the sources that would mention your activities. _____

    _____

4. Look at your responses for questions 1–3. Judging from this evidence, what conclusions or inferences could future historians make about your day?

    _____

    _____

5. Why is it important to create written records? _____

    _____

BONUS

The Age of Exploration

The Age of Exploration began in the fifteenth century and lasted about 200 years. These years were rich with discovery. Explorers traveled in their search for gold, more trade partners, and the Fountain of Youth. Set sail through the grid below by coloring the boxes with names of explorers from this time in history.

Christopher Columbus	Vasco da Gama	Julius Caesar	Amelia Earhart	Colonel Sanders
Guccio Gucci	Samuel de Champlain	Juan Ponce de León	Sir Francis Drake	Elizabeth Windsor
Abraham Lincoln	Drake Francis	Dr. Martin Luther King, Jr.	John Cabot	Paul Revere
Clara Barton	Ulysses S. Grant	Samuel Hudson	Marco Polo	Benjamin Franklin
George Washington	Arthur Ashe	Harriet Tubman	Amerigo Vespucci	Leif Eriksson

Renaissance Men and Women

The word *renaissance* means "rebirth" or "rediscovery." The Renaissance era, which followed the Middle Ages, marked great cultural change, particularly in the fields of science, the arts, religion, and architecture. Following are the names of some of the great leaders in their fields during the Renaissance. Write their names in the correct categories below. Then, research and write three facts about one of the people on the lines provided.

Blaise Pascal	Catherine de Medici	Dante Alighieri
Elizabeth I	Galileo Galilei	Geoffrey Chaucer
Henry VII	Thomas More	Isaac Newton
Johannes Gutenberg	John Calvin	Leonardo da Vinci
Martin Luther	Michelangelo	Nicolaus Copernicus
Peter Henlein	Raphael Santi	William Shakespeare

1. artists

_____
_____
_____

2. scientists

_____
_____
_____

3. writers

_____
_____
_____

4. religious leaders

_____
_____
_____

5. royalty

_____
_____
_____

6. inventors

_____
_____
_____

_____

_____

_____

_____

_____

BONUS

Take It Outside!

Go for a walk around your neighborhood. Take a pen and a notebook with you. Periodically pause and write notes about what you have done, seen, and heard. Review your notes when you return home. Then, write a 50-word summary about your walk. Next, edit your summary to 30 words. Be sure to keep the main ideas. Can you edit your writing to a 20- or 10-word summary?

Contact the water treatment facility for your community. Find out when tours are offered. Schedule a time with a family member to take the tour. Bring a pen and a notebook. Highlight the steps in the process of treating the water for community consumption. After the tour, make a chart showing the process. Share the procedural chart with friends. Also, write a note to the water treatment facility, highlighting what you learned and thanking them for their time spent giving you the tour.

Visit the library or go online to do some research about the shortage of clean drinking water in many of the world's developing countries. What sorts of problems does a lack of clean water cause? What solutions are being used to supply people in these nations with drinkable water?

Talk with a family member about scheduling a time to go to a local sporting event. Think of the many people it takes to organize and host a game or match. When the date arrives, bring a pen and a notebook with you. Pay attention to the various people who work at the event, as well as the participants and spectators. After attending the game, write a paragraph about the people who were there and the roles they played.

Section 1

Day 1/Page 3: 1. 5,233; 2. 33; 3. 49,378; 4. 64.746;
5. 177,261; 6. 2,473,515; 7. 1.38; 8. 154.66; 9. 1,578; 10.
329.57; 11. 1.3; 12. 0.65; 13.–18. Green letters should
be circled.13. ig**no**ble, not noble or honorable;
14. **spe**cious, having a false look of being fair
or right; 15. **er**satz, an imitation that is not as
good as the original; 16. de**ba**cle, a complete
disaster; 17. col**la**teral, related but of secondary
importance; 18. de**mean**, to lower in character
or status; 19. the act of punishing; 20. to vanish;
21. to soak before; 22. to wind again; 23. without
color; 24. not sure; 5, 4, 1, 3, 2, 6

Day 2/Page 5: 1. $3^5 = 243$; 2. $7^2 = 49$; 3. $4^4 = 256$;
4. $2^6 = 64$; 5. $9^3 = 729$; 6. $10^8 = 100,000,000$; 7. $5^4 =$
625; 8. $8^4 = 4,096$; 9. $6^3 = 216$; 10. C; 11. F; 12. R; 13. C;
14. F; 15.–16. Answers will vary.; 17. C; 18. C; 19. A;
20. A; 21. A; 17.–21. Words will vary.; 22. C; 23. F;
24. E; 25. D; 26. B; 27. I; 28. H; 29. G; 30. A

Day 3/Page 7: 1.–8. Answers will vary.; 9. 3; 10. 5;
11. 8; 12. 48; 13. 9; 14. 12; 15. 15; 16. 9; Earth's crust is
broken into huge pieces called tectonic plates.
These plates include whole continents and
sections of the ocean floor. Tectonic plates **are**
shifting constantly. The uneven line where two
plates meet is called a rift zone. **Earthquakes**
often occur along rift zones. When part of
a slowly moving plate **sticks** to an opposing
plate at a point along the rift zone, pressure
builds. The pressure rises behind the section
until finally it gives way and moves. The shock
from this sudden shift is like a stone tossed into
a pond. It sends waves in all directions.; 17.
C; 18. being careful about how much energy
you use and trying to use less energy; 19. You
could travel farther using less fuel.; 20. plastic,
glass, paper, and metal; 21. turn off lights
when leaving a room, unplug appliances and
machines when everyone will be gone

Day 4/Page 9: 1. 6; 2. 5; 3. 8; 4. 7; 5. 7; 6. 3; 7. 9; 8.
4; 9. 5; 10. S; 11. H; 12. S; 13. P; 14. M; 15. M; 16. P; 17. P;
18. S; 19. H; 20. B; 21. A; 22. C; 23. C; 24. A; 20.–24.
Words will vary.; Students' writing will vary.

Day 5/Page 11:

Nuts (x)	Fruit (y)
3	1
6	2
9	3
12	4
15	5

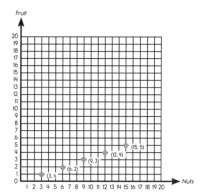

1. Gretchen, can you give me a hand?; 2. The
mural was filled with splashes of blue, green,
gold, and red.; 3. Mrs. Yim, my fourth-grade
teacher, was always my favorite.; 4. You can
either come to my house, or I will come to
yours.; 5. Carla donated food, blankets, and
clothing.; 6. "Please show me the way out
of here," said Mia.; 7. I want to leave, but I
am afraid that I will miss something.; 8. On
Saturday, April 18, 2009, I went swimming
in Crystal Creek.; 9. prefix–mis–, root word–
fortune; 10. prefix–re–, root word–move; 11.
root word–pain, suffix––less; 12. prefix–un–, root
word–usual; 13. prefix–dis–, root word–appear

Day 6/Page 13: 1. 6; 2. 8; 3. 15; 4. 12; 5. 24; 6. 30; 7.
30; 8. 36; 9. 28; 10.–18. Students should circle the
words in green: 10. **The robin** is considered a
sign of spring in the Midwest.; 11. **The Henderson
family** moved into an apartment on the 14th
floor.; 12. **I** read about the extra traffic that
creates problems during the winter.; 13. **The US
Open** is a prestigious tennis tournament.; 14.
Each member of the team deserves a trophy
for his participation and hard work.; 15. **Some
rivers** flow in a northern direction.; 16. **Chang's
family** went hiking in Yellowstone National
Park.; 17. **Kelsey** adopted the tiny gray kitten
from the animal shelter.; 18. **Nora, Quinn, and
Scott** are going to the pool this afternoon.;
19.–23. Answers may vary. Possible answers: 19.
Sam, a helicopter pilot, goes out one snowy
night to rescue Boy Scouts who are stuck on a
mountain.; 20. No, he doesn't let her know that
he is concerned because he doesn't want to
worry her.; 21. felt a wave of worry wash over
him; 22. Isobel is someone accustomed to the
nature of Sam's job, but she still worries about
his safety. In the beginning, she says, "Who is it
this time?" and then she questions Sam about
the safety of the rescue.; 23. Answers will vary.

Day 7/Page 15: 1. $\frac{1}{9}$, $\frac{3}{9}$; 2. $\frac{2}{6}$, $\frac{1}{6}$; 3. $\frac{25}{30}$,

$\frac{12}{30}$; 4. $\frac{9}{24}$, $\frac{16}{24}$; 5. $\frac{3}{9}$, $\frac{4}{9}$; 6. $\frac{36}{45}$, $\frac{25}{45}$; 7. $\frac{14}{28}$,

$\frac{12}{28}$; 8. $\frac{16}{24}$, $\frac{21}{24}$; 9. $\frac{18}{30}$, $\frac{25}{30}$; 10. Some, are;
11. gate, is; 12. Tucson, lies; 13. statue, stands; 14.
Dodgers, Braves, Cardinals, are; 15.–19. Answers
will vary.; 20. prefix–mis–, root word–spell,
suffix––ed; 21. prefix–dis–, root word–agree; 22.
prefix–re–, root word–appear, suffix––ing; 23.
root word–hope, suffix––less; 24. prefix–un–,
root word–like, suffix––ly; 25. too funny for
words; 26. small world after all; 27. deep in
thought; 28. broken promise

Day 8/Page 17:

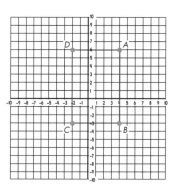

D (–2, 6); 1.–5. Proverb meanings may vary.
Possible answers: 1. hand, Having something
certain is better than taking a risk for
something you might not get.; 2. fonder, When
you are away from someone, you appreciate
them more. 3. cloud, Something good can be
found, even in bad situations.; greener, The
things that other people have always look
better than what you have. ; 5. Actions, The
way you act is more meaningful than the
things you say.; 6. social blunder; 7. street that
is closed at one end; 8. summary of a person's
accomplishments; 9. strength; 10. C; 11. D; 12. F;
13. A; 14. I; 15. E; 16. H; 17. B; 18. G

Day 9/Page 19: 1. 132; 2. 1,159.58; 3. 187; 4. 1,284; 5.
132.16; 6. 9,802.33; 7. 2,021; 8. 5,808.6; 9. 13,878.2;
Every Monday, students in Mrs. Verdan's class
work in pairs to complete math challenges.
Each pair selects its own working space.
Gregory and Lea **like** the table by the window.
Lily and Masandra **take** the round table near
the door. Mandy and Zoe **grab** the soft seats
in the library corner. Each pair has 45 minutes
to solve the puzzle. Most of them **finish** on time.
They **share** their solutions with the whole class.
Mrs. Verdan explains the solution and answers
questions. Mrs. Verdan's students **enjoy** the

weekly math challenges.; 10. B; 11. a Babylonian king who created the first set of laws; 12. so everyone in the kingdom would know what laws to obey; 13. a large slab of stone that was posted for all to see; 14. Answers will vary.

Day 10/Page 21: 1. 30 bottles of water; 2. 10 inches; 3. 420 miles; 4. 15 points; 5. between *calorie* and *digestion*; 6. A; 7. Possible answers: proteins and fats; 8. a measure of the energy stored in food; 9. mug, gum; 10. diaper, repaid; 11. loop, pool; 12. tide, edit; 13. flow, wolf; Comic strips will vary.

Day 11/Page 23: 1. –7, –5, –2, 0, 3, 7; 2. –5, –3, –2, 2, 3, 4; 3. –12, –1, 0, 5, 10, 11; 4. –8, –3, –2, 2, 5, 12; 5. 24; 6. 35; 7. 56; 8. 82; 9. 16; 10. 39; 11. $\frac{3}{8}$; 12. $\frac{8}{7}$; 13. $\frac{7}{11}$; 14. $\frac{4}{5}$; 15. $\frac{5}{16}$; 16. $\frac{7}{12}$; 17. flare; 18. smog; 19. crunch; 20. motel; 21. glimmer; 22. compass rose; 23. title; 24. legend; 25. scale

Day 12/Page 25: 1. 9.68; 2. 60.7; 3. 188.2; 4. 88.267; 5. 4.41; 6. 27.99; 7. 11.19; 8. 7.29; 9. 206.9; 10. 65.65; 11. 7.65; 12. 22.396; 13. A; 14. A; 15. C; 16. A; 17. C; 18. A; 19. C; 20. C; Pride is an abstract noun. Explanations will vary.; 21. B; 22. A; 23. A; 24. B; 25. B; Students' writing will vary.

Day 13/Page 27: 1. 9 feet; 2. 80 cups; 3. 2 yards; 4. 80 ounces; 5. 84 inches; 6. 8 yards; 7. 5 gallons; 8. 4 quarts; 9. 144 inches; 10. 3 pounds; 11.–15. Answers will vary. Possible answers: 11. Although I don't like raw tomatoes, I do like spaghetti sauce.; 12. Mia brought spinach and artichoke dip to the potluck.; 13. Darren went to the pool at 10:00, and he went for a bike ride with Treyvon after lunch.; 14. Rebecca and Natalia play soccer on Tuesdays at 4:30.; 15. Uncle Ned picked peppers and tomatoes from his garden.; 16. *Land of Treasure* at Theater Town; 17. B; 18. Cinema 6

Day 14/Page 29: 1. 324; 2. Phillip—108 peanuts, Joy—54 peanuts, Brent—81 peanuts, Preston—10 peanuts; 3. Sidney couldn't do **anything** with her hair.; 4. Mateo didn't have **any** second thoughts about the decision he made.; 5. No, Celia didn't see **anyone** else at the market.; 6. Kevin could not **ever** see the road because of the heavy snow.; 7. Mia hasn't received **any** mail in more than a week.; 8. I didn't borrow **any** of the movies from Toni.; 9. A; 10. B; 11. A; 12. B; 13. A; Students' writing will vary.

Day 15/Page 31: 1. 100 – (y × 12) = 16 when y =

7; 2. b × (15 + 37) = 156 when b = 3; 3. 27 + (z × 12) = 87 when z = 5; 4. 135 ÷ (c × 5) = 3 when c = 9; 5. w^2 × (12 ÷ 4) = 300 when w = 10; 6. (12 × d) ÷ (25 – 19) = 4 when d = 2; 7. (x × 5) + 13 = 68 when x = 11; 8. neighbor, her; 9. guests, their; 10. lawyer, her; 11. Students, their; 12. anyone, he or she; 13. girl, her; 14. members, their; 15. B; 16. A; 17. B; 18. A; 19. A

Day 16/Page 33: 1. 15a; 2. 18x – 24; 3. 9g + 108; 4. 3w^2 – 8w; 5. 50 + 20m; 6. 39z; 7. 9y + 21; 8. 5b + 100; 9. 32c + 48; 10. 72d; 11. 7n^2 + 56; 12. 40 ÷ 18f; 13. I, our; 14. you, me, their; 15. his, her; 16. she, us; 17. me, it; 18. We, it, your; 19. I; 20. them; 21. we; 22. her, her; 23. C; 24. Its remains have turned to stone.; 25. bones, teeth, and/or shell; 26. to learn what the living animals or plants looked like; 27. All living things contain carbon, so scientists measure how much carbon is left in a fossil to determine its age.

Day 17/Page 35: 1. Dependent variable: total price of the oranges, Independent variable: number of pounds bought, Equation: $1.15 × number of pounds = total cost of oranges; 2. Dependent variable: total height, Independent variable: number of months, Equation: 24 + (6 × number of months) = total height; 3.–12. Students should circle the words in green. 3. **Their** → mom; 4. **Our** → house; 5. **Its** → handle; 6. **mine** → dog; 7. **Her** → socks; 8. **his** → parents; 9. **his** → house; 10. **My** → friend, **my** → opinion; 11. **hers** → sandwich; 12. **Their** → backyard; 13. N, barren; 14. P, calm; 15. P, honorable; 16. N, to mislead or abandon; 17. P, fearless; 18. Ireland; 19. Russia; 20. Germany; 21. Austria; 22. Denmark; 23. Turkey; 24. Sweden; 25. Latvia; 26. Portugal; 27. Belarus

Day 18/Page 37: 1. 26; 2. 5; 3. 3; 4. 20; 5. 13; 6. 188; 7. 5; 8. 125; 9. Many; 10. others; 11. Someone; 12. few, several; 13. somebody; 14. either; 15. Anybody; 16. each; 17. both; 18. Some, others; 19. P, spends money carefully, N, stingy, unwilling to spend money; 20. N, fussy; P, specific about what is wanted; 21. N, aggressive; P, bold, confident; 22. N, disdainful, arrogant, P, feeling satisfied as a result of an achievement; 23. both; 24. plant; 25. both; 26. plant; 27. animal; 28. plant; 29. both; 30. animal; 31. both

Day 19/Page 39: 1. y = 3; 2. x = 16; 3. v = 10; 4. m = 17; 5. q = 115; 6. r = 56; 7. w = 8; 8. z = 36; 9. a = 42; 10. y = 8; 11. g = 60; 12. c = 5; 13. herself; 14. themselves; 15. myself; 16. himself; 17. yourself;

18. himself; 19. itself; 20. myself; 21. polyps; 22. off the coast of northeast Australia; 23. B, C; 24. having too many organisms living in an area; 25. people visiting the reef, changes in the environment, and harmful animals; 26. The author thinks the Great Barrier Reef is a natural treasure that should be protected. This can be seen in phrases such as "wonders of the world," "fragile," and "carelessness."

Day 20/Page 41: 1. Lowest value: 77, Highest value: 99, Spread: 22, Center value: 88; 2. Lowest value: 24, Highest value: 84, Spread: 60, Center value: 52; 3. Lowest value: 9, Highest value: 22, Spread: 13, Center value: 15; **Whoever** forgot to return the scissors should bring **them** back to the art room. A few pairs were missing from the room after our meeting. In the future, **no one** will be allowed to remove supplies from the room. The school trusts us, and we have a responsibility to leave the workspace as we found **it**. I am sure that **this** was a mistake. That is why I am asking each member to check **his or her** backpack. Call me if you find **them**. Thank you for **your** help!; 4. ~~hardly~~; 5. ~~no~~, any; 6. ~~more~~; 7. ~~good~~, well; 8. ~~tallest~~, taller; 9. ~~more~~, most; 10. ~~hardly~~; 11. ~~gooder~~, better; 12. ~~most~~; 13. ~~more~~; Students' writing will vary.

Bonus Page 43: Results and answer will vary.

Bonus Page 44: 1. Answers will vary.; 2. The coin moves with the card and does not fall into the cup.; 3. When the card is pulled quickly, the coin slides over the card. There is little friction between the card and the coin. The coin is not affected by the movement of the card. Gravity pulls the coin into the cup.; 4. Answers will vary.

Bonus Page 45:
1. Anchorage; 2. Atlanta; 3. Chicago; 4. Denver; 5. Seattle; 6. Phoenix; 7. San Diego; 8. New York City; 9. Ottawa; 10. Vancouver

Bonus Page 46: Across: 3. Athena; 4. Zeus; 5. Hera; 7. Demeter; 9. Ares; 11. Poseidon; 12. Hypnos: Down: 1. Hades; 2. Hermes; 3. Aphrodite; 6. Apollo; 8. Gaea; 10. Chronos

Bonus Page 47: From left to right and top to bottom, drawings should be labeled: 4, 1, 7, 2, 3, 5, 8, 6; 1. China;

2. United States; 3. Egypt; 4. India; 5. Italy; 6. England; 7. France; 8. Mexico

Day 1/Page 51: 1. $\frac{1}{9}$ cubic ft.; 2. $\frac{39}{512}$ cubic in.; 3. $\frac{7}{384}$ cubic cm; 4. $\frac{1}{12}$ cubic cm; 5. $\frac{3}{25}$ cubic m; 6. $\frac{3}{8}$ cubic yd.; 7. Miller's Farm Stand (the one off of Route 82) has the best watermelons this time of year.; 8. We watched the ball soar—right over the fence—and land on Mr. Wilson's deck.; 9. My friend Emily, the girl I met at camp, taught me the funniest joke.; 10. After hiking all day—almost halfway up a mountain—, I fell asleep as soon as my head hit the pillow.; 11. Romana's has a special today on my favorite pizza (mushroom, pepper, and bacon).; 12. *Escape From Space* (starring Ethan Myers) was my favorite movie of the summer.; 13. as fit as a fiddle → Mom, Mom feels well again.; 14. as smart as a fox → detective, The detective was very crafty.; 15. like sunshine on a cloudy day → smile, Her smile is welcome and bright.; 16. like thunder → footsteps, His footsteps were very loud.; 17. 60%; 18. 90%; 19. 13%; 20. 89%; 21. $\frac{1}{25}$; 22. $\frac{4}{25}$; 23. $\frac{1}{4}$; 24. $\frac{17}{50}$

Day 2/Page 53: From left to right and top to bottom: 1. 36, 34, 41, 10; 2. 16, 10, 10, 27; 3. 15, 14, 14, 22; 4. 42, 41, 41, 66; 5.–14. Students should circle the words in orange: 5. is pouring; 6. had scurried; 7. are going; 8. can be dimmed; 9. was taking; 10. must have tried; 11. would be; 12. had flown; 13. should pull; 14. may have been going; 15. C; 16. from AD 1350 to AD 1600; 17. People began rereading the ancient texts and creating new art, literature, and architecture.; 18. His plays are still performed today.; 19. art, architecture, and science; 20. These terms have a positive connotation because they mean that someone is good at many different things.

Day 3/Page 55: 1. 7; 2. 2; 3. 2; 4. 13$\frac{1}{2}$; 5. 6$\frac{2}{3}$; 6. 8$\frac{3}{4}$; 7. 1; 8. $\frac{1}{2}$; 9. $\frac{3}{10}$; 10. Students conducted experiments to test the hypothesis.; 11. More than two-thirds of the applicants passed the exam.; 12. The choir sings the song at every graduation.; 13. All of my friends enjoyed the vegetarian pizza.; 14. Cameron hammered the nail into the wall.; 15. test, piece of cake, The test was easy.; 16. Winning, dream come true, Winning was like a dream.; 17. backyard, blanket of snow, The backyard was covered with snow.; 18. pillow, cloud, The pillow was soft and fluffy.; 19. lake, mirror, The lake was smooth and reflective.; 20. 0.3; 21. 1.2; 22. 12.8; 23. 6.48; 24. 4.8; 25. 8.1; 26. 5.44; 27. 6.75; 28. 38.44; 29.

16; 30. 6; 31. 18.87

Day 4/Page 57: 1. $23.20, $34.80; 2. $38.40, $89.60; 3. $2.40, $13.60; 4. $456.00, $304.00; 5. $10.45, $8.55; 6. $45.00, $55.00; 7. $625.00, $1,875.00;

Once a month, our school **holds** a game day in the gymnasium. We participate in races and other games. Fernando and Melvin always **race** on the same team. They **enjoy** running. Target toss is a favorite event. Each player **tosses** the ball at a target painted on the wall. Laura and Jordana usually win because they **practice** after school. José and Luke like basketball. Kyle and Spencer usually **score** more points, but José and Luke **are** improving all of the time. At the end of the day, teams from two classes play a game of volleyball.; 8. part/whole; 9. cause/effect; 10. item/category; 11. item/category; 12. part/whole; 13. cause/effect

Day 5/Page 59: 1. 4; 2. 1$\frac{3}{25}$; 3. 1$\frac{9}{25}$; 4. $\frac{3}{4}$; 5. 2; 6. 3$\frac{1}{3}$; 7. 6$\frac{2}{3}$; 8. 4$\frac{1}{2}$; 9. 1$\frac{1}{5}$; 10.–19. Students should circle the words in orange. 10. gushed, water; 11. chews, gum; 12. kicked, door; 13. handed, paper; 14. stowed, luggage; 15. offered, carrots; 16. canceled, subscription; 17. crochets, blanket; 18. made, soup; 19. toasted, marshmallow; 20. harmful to living things; 21. She felt it was important to keep toxic chemicals away from crops and animals.; 22. wildlife and marine biology

Day 6/Page 61: 1. 69, 70, 76, 80, 80, 81, 87, 90, 91, 94, 95; 2. 60, 68, 68, 68, 74, 74, 75, 75, 77, 81; 3.–11. Students should circle the words in orange: 3. gave, puppy; 4. wished, grandmother; 5. sold, Yow; 6. handed, Kent; 7. offered, Tommy; 8. knitted, June; 9. gave, chair; 10. wrote, state representative; 11. brought, family; 12. All roads lead to Rome.; 13. between a rock and a hard place; 14. on the tip of your tongue; 15. in one ear and out the other; 16. bite off more than you can chew; Students' writing will vary.

Day 7/Page 63: 1. 95.2; 2. 80.6; 3. 240.5; 4. 2.38; 5. 13.52; 6. 4.368; 7. 25,115.8; 8. 291.928; 9. 7.74; 10. 22.248; 11. 3,644.8; 12. 180.471; 13. 37%; 14. 69%; 15. 40%; 16. 21%; 17. 99.9%; 18. 49.9%; 19. 175%; 20. 225%; 21. 0.24; 22. 0.65; 23. 0.88; 24. 0.03; 25. 0.17; 26. 0.09; 27. 0.1; 28. 0.86; 29. Fortune is given the ability to smile.; 30. The clock is given the ability to sing.; 31. Wind is given the ability to whistle.; 32. Daisies are given emotions.; 33. The weather is given the ability to grant permission.; 34. 54;

35. 200; 36. 18; 37. 30; 38. 24; 39. 17.5

Day 8/Page 65: 1. 22.5 miles; 2. $4.10; 3. $5.60; 4. 43.8 meters; Woofer—that silly dog—is home again. I called—actually, whistled—for Woofer to come to dinner. Usually, he runs into the kitchen, but the house was quiet. I didn't know where he could be. I was searching for Woofer when Carol—my older sister—came home from school. When I told her that Woofer was missing, she helped me look in every room—even under the beds. We couldn't find Woofer. Carol asked Mrs. Linden—the retired teacher next door—if she had seen him. Then, Nicholas—Carol's friend—walked up the street with Woofer trotting behind him.; 5. the sound made by the air as the lightning heats it; 6. because light travels faster than sound; 7. D; 8. the amount of energy released

Day 9/Page 67: 1. 22.7; 2. 2.25; 3. 4.91; 4. 0.021; 5. 20.1; 6. 2.01; 7. 0.61; 8. 0.46; 9. mean=16.1, median=16.5, range=15, mode=22; 10. 25%; 11. 30%; 12. conflict; 13. allusion; 14. dialogue; 15. hyperbole; 16. foreshadowing; 17. point of view; 18. setting; 19. irony; 20. imagery; Students' writing will vary.

Day 10/Page 69: 1. 9; 2. 0.2; 3. 9.9; 4. 0.8; 5. 6.2; 6. 7; 7. 0.5; 8. 0.8; 9. The appointments available are 12:00 P.M.–4:00 P.M.; 10. The assignment for tomorrow is to read pages 24–36 carefully.; 11. The Chicago–New York flight lasts less than two hours.; 12. We go to great lengths—often far beyond our normal limitations—to win!; 13. If I only needed to read chapters 2–4, I would be finished by now.; 14. Camper One enjoys waking up at Frog Pond.; 15. Camper Two is irritated when waking up at Frog Pond.; 16. Answers will vary.; 17.–24. Answers may vary. Possible answers: 17. A, childish; 18. C, antivirus; 19. B, neighborhood; 20. C, submarine; 21. A, intercostal; 22. A, happily; 23. C, harden; 24. B, semicircle

Day 11/Page 71: 1. $\frac{13}{32}$ cups of sugar in each batch; 2. 1$\frac{17}{20}$ miles each hour; 3. $\frac{118\frac{1}{8}}{15}=\frac{y}{1}$ 7$\frac{7}{8}$ gallons each minute; 4.–8. Answers will vary. Possible answers: 4. While I was putting on my pajamas, my sister fell asleep.; 5. While I was laughing at the show on TV, my glass of milk spilled.; 6. While I was walking to school, a tiny, mewing kitten caught my attention.; 7. After I quickly changed my clothes, Mom told me to set the table for dinner.; 8. Though Megan's sister was only 4 years old, Megan taught her to read.; 9.–11.

Answers may vary. Possible answers: 9. The story is told by someone who is new to the house or school. He is taking everything in and observing all the details.; 10. The story seems to take place a long time ago. The language the author uses seems old-fashioned (*amusements, chamber, pitchers of milk*).The children are also occupied with old-fashioned activities, like marbles, checkers, and sliding down banisters.; 11. The author includes so many details and examples that I can see the house clearly in my mind. It seems very warm and busy with the activities of all the children.; 12. tempting, enticing

Day 12/Page 73:

1. 30; 2. 21; 3. 35; On August 2, 1971, Commander David R. Scott stood **proudly** on the surface of the moon. As the cameras rolled, the astronaut **dramatically** dropped a feather and a hammer. On Earth, the hammer would fall much **faster**. **Amazingly**, the two objects landed on the moon's surface at the same time. **Unbelievably**, Galileo Galilei had **accurately** predicted the results of this experiment **nearly** 400 years earlier. A legend claims that Galileo **boldly** dropped a cannonball and a musket ball from the Leaning Tower of Pisa in Pisa, Italy, to test his theory, but few modern historians **actually** believe the tale.; 4. The Field Museum in Chicago, Illinois, in the present; 5. on a wagon train in the United States, in the past; 6. a school, in the future; Students' writing will vary.

Day 13/Page 75: 1. –4; 2. 29; 3. –11; 4. 8; 5. –13; 6. –21; 7. $3\frac{53}{72}$; 8. $1\frac{1}{12}$; 9. $6\frac{13}{14}$; 10. $4\frac{8}{9}$; 11. $1\frac{59}{60}$; 12. $4\frac{1}{28}$; 13. D; 14. I; 15. I; 16. D; 17. I; 18. D; 19. Lena wrapped the gifts and hid them before her mom came home.; 20. Boseley raced across the yard, hoping to finally catch the pesky squirrel.; 21. Samantha made it to the regional spelling bee because she studied hard for months.; 22. On the first Thursday of every month, our book group meets for snacks and a discussion of our latest book.; 23. Although

we forgot to hang our food from a tree, the bears and raccoons did not raid our campsite overnight.; The monarch butterflies will have a place to lay eggs. The caterpillars will have food to eat.; The bird survived. The net was disposed of properly so that no other animals could get caught in it.

Day 14/Page 77: 1. 240 times; 2. 19 times; 3. 6 times; 4. Skiing and hiking; 5. Saving his money 6. taking both piano and voice lessons; 7. Cleaning out the chicken coop; 8. cleaning her room; 9. to achieve our personal best; 10. to stop the leak; 11. to impress her parents; 12. To be a good listener; 13. to weed the garden before lunch; 14. a river where a large deposit of gold was found; 15. a year's worth of supplies; 16. stock up on food, tools, and clothing for the journey; 17. Western Canada and the Pacific Northwest of the United States; 18. Answers will vary.

Day 15/Page 79: 1. $4x + 11$; 2. $3y + 1$; 3. $2a + 4$; 4. $3x + 5$; 5. $6y - 6$; 6. $3b + 3$; 7. $3(4y - 1)$; 8. $4x(x - 3)$; 9.–$3(3c - 1)$; 10.–14. Answers will vary. Possible answers: 10. I lost my wallet on Friday., Sarah misplaced her keys.; 11. What a unique piece of art!, That was such an odd comment for Harold to make.; 12. Chloe could not stop smelling the awful odor all day., The aroma of freshly baked bread drifted through the house.; 13. I just wanted to stare at my brand-new baby sister all day long.; Jorge tried to glower at his mom so she would know how annoyed he was.; 14. The pushy girl tried to cut in line, but no one would let her., Sam is confident that the Hawks will win the game on Saturday.; 15. planets and stars; 16. Both are objects in outer space, are bright specks in the night sky, and are far from Earth. Planets can be solid or made of gas, get light from the sun, and can be any temperature. Stars are balls of hot gases, produce their own light, and are extremely hot.; 17. E; 18. D; 19. E; 20. A; 21. D; 22. B; 23. C; 24. B or E; 25. C; 26. A; 27. F

Day 16/Page 81: 1. 384 cm²; 512 cm³; 2. 136.95 square miles; 3. 15,552 in.³; 33 cans of paint; 4. 1,687.5 cm²; 5. 196 ft.³; auto = self; spec = see; ped = foot; aqua = water; ject = throw; scrib/script = write; port = carry; mono = one; 6. biographies and mysteries; 7. Both are types of books. Biographies tell facts about a person's life, while mysteries are usually fictional.; 8. D; 9. B; 10. A; 11. C; 12. F; 13. E

Day 17/Page 83: 1. $\frac{1}{6}$; 2. $\frac{5}{6}$; 3. $\frac{7}{18}$; 4. $\frac{5}{9}$; 5. $\frac{4}{9}$; 6. $\frac{5}{9}$; 7. $\frac{1}{6}$; 8. $\frac{1}{3}$; 9. $\frac{1}{2}$; 10. $\frac{5}{6}$; 11. $\frac{1}{2}$; 12. $\frac{2}{3}$; 13. Romeo; refers to the play *Romeo and Juliet* by Shakespeare, a male who is very romantic/popular with girls; 14. Pandora's box; refers to a Greek myth, a place where dangerous secrets are kept; 15. Hercules; refers to the name of a hero from Greek mythology, someone very strong; 16. Einstein; refers to the famous scientist Albert Einstein, someone who is very intelligent, especially at science; 17. Pinocchio's; refers to the fairy tale, someone who often lies; 18. The Rosetta Stone was found in Egypt more than 200 years ago.; 19. There are three kinds of writing on the stone.; 20. The Rosetta Stone unlocked the mystery of ancient Egyptian symbols.; 21. B

Day 18/Page 85: 1. 20, 23, 26; 2. 66, 61, 56; 3. 60, 52, 44; 4. 50, 55, 65; 5. 57, 54, 51; 6. 657, 742, 827; 7. 95, 131, 173; 8. 172, 154, 136; 9. 36, 49, 64; 10. 32, 64, 128; 11. preposition; 12. verb; 13. noun; 14. adverb; 15. proper noun; 16. conjunction; 17. adjective; 18. verb; 19. pronoun; 20. article; 21. logical; 22. Carrying an umbrella does not make it rain.; 23. logical; 24. B; 25. A; 26. E; 27. C; 28. D; 29. F

Day 19/Page 87: 1. 44 green marbles; 2. 540 students; 3. 160 sixth graders; 4. 30 small shirts, 90 medium shirts, and 130 large shirts; 5. My sisters stood in line for 45 minutes to buy tickets for the concert.; 6. Eli made the muffins with a lemon glaze for his mom.; 7. The art teacher said that she would return our projects on Thursday.; 8. The girl's gorgeous photograph won first place in the show.; 9. 2; 10. 3; 11. 3; 12. 2; 13. 1; 14. 3; 15. 2; 16. 3; 17. 2; 18. 1; 19. 2; 20. 1; Students' writing will vary.

Day 20/Page 89: parentheses, exponents, multiplication and division, addition and subtraction; 1. 14; 2. 30; 3. 33; 4. 8; 5. 11; 6. 3; 7. D; 8. I; 9. I; 10. D; 11. I; 12. D; 13. I; 14. D; 15. A; 16. animals and mythical creatures; 17. because they are closer to Earth; 18. International Astronomical Union; 19. Summaries will vary.

Bonus Page 91: 1. The pencil appears to be broken or bent at the point it enters the water.; 2. The objects appear to be in different locations, depending from which angle they are viewed.; 3. The beam of light appears to bend as it enters the water. It scatters into a larger beam.

Section III

Day 1/Page 99: 1. 21; 2. –12; 3. –5; 4. 8; 5. –10; 6. –75; 7. $13\frac{5}{87}$; 8. $2\frac{19}{30}$; 9. $13\frac{3}{10}$; 10. $11\frac{28}{45}$; 11. $19\frac{1}{3}$; 12. $8\frac{7}{22}$; 13. E; 14. D; 15. F; 16. C; 17. B; 18. A; 19. G; 20.–21. Answers will vary.; 22. hard; 23. area next to an ocean or a sea; 24. up-to-date; 25. company; 26. glide downhill; 27. swiftest part of a stream; Students' writing will vary.

Day 2/Page 101: 1. 0.875, T; 2. 0.6667, R; 3. 0.5556, R; 4. 0.8333, R; 5. 0.4375, T; 6. 0.5833, R; 7.–12. Students should circle the words in blue: 7. **Corn, green beans**; 8. entertained, excited; 9. cooked, ate; 10. **Diana, I**; 11. sipped, played; 12. **Vanilla, butter pecan**; 13.–14. Answers will vary.;

Racing $\left\{\begin{array}{l}\text{red}\\\text{black}\\\text{silver}\end{array}\right.$ Mountain $\left\{\begin{array}{l}\text{red}\\\text{black}\\\text{silver}\end{array}\right.$

15. 6; 16. $\frac{1}{2}$; 17. $\frac{1}{3}$; 18. $\frac{1}{6}$; Students' writing will vary.

Day 3/Page 103: 1. X; 2. X; 3. X; 4. ✔; 5. X; 6. ✔; 7. X; 8. ✔; 9. m = 4; 10. a = 1; 11. d = 4; 12. n = 14; 13. p = 18; 14. j = 2; 15. s = 20; 16. y = 9; 17. r = 1; 18. k = 36; 19. g = 24; 20. t = 7; 21. C; 22. people's ages, occupations, educational levels, and incomes; 23. to determine the makeup of a city's or county's population and whether there is a need for different services; 24. by taking a national census; 25. The Canadian government takes a census every 5 years. The United States government takes a census every 10 years.

Day 4/Page 105: 1. 6.25 minutes per mile, 4.45 minutes per mile, Brie runs faster.; 2. $3.85 per pound, $4.21 per pound, Lucy got the better deal.; 3. 260 calories per hour, 291 calories per hour, Zack burned more calories per hour.; Camille's best friend is Marcella. They're in different classes this year, but they've known each other since preschool. They haven't spent more than a few days apart in their lives. Marcella's mom is Camille's father's boss. Marcella's father is Camille's uncle's business partner. The two families' friendship has lasted more than 15 years. Marcella has two older brothers, and Camille has one. They're in high school now, but they'll be in college soon. The boys' relationship is very close too. They don't hesitate to call one another for advice.; 4. D; 5. A; 6. D; 7. C; 8. D

Day 5/Page 107: 1. –35; 2. –8; 3. 27; 4. –5; 5. –63; 6. 18; 7. $10\frac{5}{24}$; 8. $3\frac{1}{7}$; 9. $6\frac{29}{36}$; 10. $4\frac{1}{21}$; 11. $3\frac{9}{10}$; 12. $17\frac{4}{21}$; 13. went faster; 14. impossible to believe; 15. overwhelming; 16. at a distance, not friendly; 17. happy and lively; 18. Animals like monkeys and sloths live in the rain forest.; 19. Some computers come in different colors.; 20. C; 21. M; 22. M; 23. C; 24. M; 25. M; 26. M; 27. C; 28. M

Day 6/Page 109: 1. equation: 18 × (12 + 15 + 18) = x, answer: $810; 2. equation: (55 × 3) – (25 × 3) = x, answer: 90 miles; 3. equation: (24 × 12) – [(24 × 12) ÷ 3] = x, answer: $192; 4. equation: x + 0.09x = (50 – 17.30), answer: $30; Jarvis is a kind, helpful, honest friend. He has short black hair and large brown, friendly eyes. When I go to Jarvis's house, we play with his dog Rover. Rover is a gentle, quiet dog. His tail is long, thin, and feathery. His ears are floppy, soft, and silky. They fly behind him when he runs. Rover is always ready to plant a big sloppy kiss on my cheek. Just like Jarvis, Rover likes everybody, and everybody likes him.; 5. B; 6. what is now the Canadian province of Newfoundland and Labrador; 7. the ruins of eight buildings built by the Vikings, and tools; 8. They had sod walls over supporting frames, and in the middle of each floor was a long, narrow fireplace.; 9. The design of the buildings and tools is similar to those found in Viking settlements in Greenland and Iceland.

Day 7/Page 111: 1. 7x + 4; 2. 12y + 20; 3. –1w – 10; 4. 2b² – 4b; 5. –27x – 63; 6. 4c – 12; 7. 5a²; 8. $\frac{12}{z}$ – 4; 9. 36d; 10. 3x + 6; 11. Morgan shouted, "Hurray! We made it!"; 12. "Have you been a part of a sports team at your school?" asked Silvia; 13. "After you take out the trash," said my dad, "we can go see a movie."; 14. Reid told Angie that "Casey at the Bat" was his favorite poem.; 15. "Look out for that bump in the road!" shouted Dad.; 16. "Leave your binoculars at home," suggested Ms. Haynes. "Your ears will be more helpful than your eyes on this field trip."; 17. "What is the quickest way to get to the park?" asked Andre.; 18. "We are going to the movies this afternoon," said Deanna, "and then we are going to get ice cream."; 19. "Be careful!" shouted Mom.; A.–C. Order of subheadings and details may vary: A. books; 1. library books; 2. reference books; 3. textbooks; B. furniture; 1. chairs; 2. desks; 3. storage cabinets; C. supplies; 1. pens; 2. pencils; 3. paper; 20. P; 21. S; 22. S; 23. P; 24. S; 25. S; 26. P; 27. P; 28. P; 29. P

Day 8/Page 113: 1. 54 + (–73) = |x|, 19; 2. 32 + 15 + (–57) = x, –10; 3. 6 + (–10) = |x|, 4; Holly Street Middle School will hold a spring program next month. I will be the announcer for the program. I will say, "The drama team is proud to present a famous story about a young woman who was too curious." After the drama team's performance, Mr. Graham's class will recite "The Cloud" by Percy Bysshe Shelley. Ms. Carrol's class will sing "The Ashe Grove."; 4. the second dog; Answers will vary.; 5. He will take a nap.; Answers will vary.

Day 9/Page 115:

x	3	6	9	12	15
y	1	2	3	4	5

k = 3

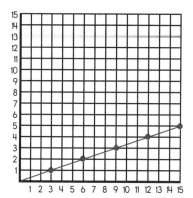

1.–4. Answers will vary. Possible answers: 1. Ana had a wonderful, unique idea for a Halloween costume., positive; 2. The flimsy toy broke after Morgan had played with it only twice., negative; 3. The Galloways plan to stay at a rustic cabin beside Lake Bellamy., neutral; 4. A tadpole is an immature frog., neutral; 5. a bird; 6. Hope is important to have during difficult times.; 7. soul/all

Day 10/Page 117: 1. 47.1 cm; 2. 18.84 yd.; 3. 40.82 ft.; 4. 6.28 m; 5. 163.28 m; 6. 389.36 ft.; 7. 226.08 yd.; 8. 401.92 mm; 9. sports-loving; 10. mother-in-law; 11. forty-four; 12. twenty-one, pitch-black; 13. Fifty-eight, late-afternoon; 14.–15. Answers will vary.; 16. B; 17. B; 16.–17. Context clues will vary.; 18. crust; 19. lithosphere; 20. asthenosphere; 21. inner core; 22. outer core; 23. mantle

Day 11/Page 119: 1. 201 cm^2; 2. 1,017 km^2; 3. 283 cm^2; 4. 201 ft.^{2}; 5. 380 cm^2; 6. 79 m^2; 7. 95 cm^2; 8. 615 in.^{2}; 9.–15. Answers will vary. Possible answers: 9. The storm was a freight train that rumbled overhead.; 10. The white sand was like powdered sugar beneath Evie's toes.; 11. The notes danced cheerfully from the strings of the violin.; 12. The patter of the raindrops was a lullaby that put Terrell to sleep.; 13. The calico cat meowed loudly, demanding that her human put down his newspaper and feed her breakfast.; 14. The summer heat was a thick, heavy blanket that covered Gabe and made him feel slow and drowsy.; 15. The old, comfortable chair welcomed Aunt Bea with comforting arms.; 16. C; 17. D; 18. B; 19. C; 20. C; 21. normal; 22. strike-slip; 23. reverse

Day 12/Page 121: 1. A = 96 cm^2; P = 40 cm; 2. A = 576 in.^{2}; P = 96 in.; 3. A = 144 ft.^{2}; P = 60 ft.; 4. A = 64 yd.^{2}; P = 40 yd.; 5. A = 280 mm^2; P = 76 mm; 6. A = 256 m^2; P = 64 m; 7.–13. Blue letters should be circled. 7. benevolent, adjective, kind and generous; 8. correlate, verb, to make a close connection with something; 9. synopsis, noun, a summary, 10. indisputably, adjective, without a doubt; 11. psoriasis, noun, a chronic skin disease; 12. abrasion, noun, a scrape; 13. amiable, adjective, friendly and pleasant; 14. Most people will never be able to see a giant panda in the wild.; 15. The exhibit has indoor and outdoor areas, and it is air-conditioned.; 16. as a symbol of friendship; 17. The author discusses the individual pandas at the National Zoo and then gives general facts about pandas. This is effective because the information about the individuals is interesting and makes readers want to know more about pandas.

Day 13/Page 123: 1. 15 m; 2. 8 m; 3. 15 cm; 4. 7 ft.; 5. Marcy forgot to bring a suitcase; Mindy remembered.; 6. So far this month, John has traveled to Jackson, Mississippi; Tallahassee, Florida; and Nashville, Tennessee.; 7. Casey looked forward to the weekend; his uncle was coming to visit.; 8. Jonah's class made lunch for Mr. Burns, the custodian; Mrs. Fry, the head cook; and Miss Bookman, the librarian.; 9. Sometimes, we stay late after practice; however, we leave when the coach goes home.; 10. A; 11. B; 12. A; 13. D; 14. A; Responses will vary.

Day 14/Page 125: 1. 5 cm; 2. 2 ft.; 3. 7 yd.; 4. 10 mm; 5. 12 in.; 6. 1 m; 7. At 3:00 P.M., everyone in class needs to take the following items to the auditorium: a pencil, an eraser, and a notebook.; 8. To Whom It May Concern:; 9. I need a few things to make a new recipe: corn, tomatoes, onions, black beans, and cilantro.; Answers will vary.; Jayla, lifeguard, truck; Judy, lawyer, motorcycle; Chuck, pilot, bike; Bill, professor, car; Students' writing will vary.

Day 15/Page 127: 1. 30; 2. 9; 3. 30; 4. 56; 5. 54 bars of soap; 6. 40 points; 7. 240 miles; 8. Mr.; 9. oz.; 10. yd.; 11. Co.; 12. Capt.; 13. in.; 14. Assoc.; 15. Ave.; 16. etc.; 17. Dr.; 18. Mrs.; 19. ft.; 20. St.; 21. lb.; 22. Jr.; 23. Inc.; 24. Sr.; 25. Blvd.; 26. U.S.; 27. Gen.; 28. Prof.; 29. stockpiles; 30. 2, 1, 3, 4; 31. April 6, 1909; 32. They helped by teaching the explorers their language and helping them plan well for the trip.

Day 16/Page 129: 1. Students should draw a trapezoid.; 2. Students should draw a regular hexagon.; 3. Students should draw a right triangle.; 4. Students should draw a square or rhombus.; 5. C; 6. S; 7. CCX; 8. S; 9. CX; 10. C; 11. CX; 12. S; 13. 3x + 21 = 45, $8; 14. 24x = 30 + 42, $3; 15. D; 16. A; 17. C; 18. E; 19. B; 20. F

Day 17/Page 131: 1. 40°, obtuse; 2. 80°, acute; 3. 90°, right; 4. 75°, acute; 5. 39°, obtuse; 6. 46°, acute; 7. 97°, obtuse; 8. 90°, right; 9. A, B; 10. A, B; 11. B, A; 12. B, A; 13. A; 14. B; 15. A; 16. A; 17. B; 18. B; 19. B; 20. B

Day 18/Page 133: 1. 90°, complementary; 2. A, supplementary; 3. 47°, 137°, 133°; 4. 48°, 42°, 138°; 5.–8. Sentences will vary.; 9. It is told in first-person point of view, from the perspective of a young horse. Using this point of view adds to the interest of the story because it's unusual to see things from the perspective of an animal.; 10. the farm where Black Beauty and his mother live; 11. He has been well-bred and comes from a line of respected horses. Hs mother thinks that the other colts are more common and haven't learned manners.; 12. Answers will vary.

Day 19/Page 135: There are 6 possible squares.; Our school newspaper (*The Bobcat Times*) took a survey last week. The results were published today. The first survey question was, "What's your favorite movie?" Two-fifths of the students preferred—big surprise—*March of the Penguins*. The girls' favorite film was *The Incredibles*; the boys' favorite was *Harry Potter and the Chamber of Secrets*. The second survey question was, "What's your favorite poem?" The sixth-grade students' favorites were the following: "Toothpaste" by Michael Rosen, "The Honey Pot" by Alan Riddell, and "Mean Song" by Eve Merriam.; 1. dictionary; 2. thesaurus; 3. atlas; 4. dictionary; 5. glossary; 6. index; 7. encyclopedia or Internet; 8. glossary; 9. atlas; 10. encyclopedia or Internet; Students' writing will vary.

Day 20/Page 137: 1. There are 2 rocks in one box, 3 rocks in another box, and 4 rocks in the last box.; 2. Three boxes have 5 seeds each. One box has 15 seeds.; 3.–12. Answers may vary. Possible answers: 3. begin; 4. absurd; 5. nourishment; 6. license; 7. meddlesome; 8. reprimand; 9. menacing; 10. think; 11. diverge; 12. puzzle; 13. B; 14. A; 15. C; 16. B; 17. demand; 18. inflation; 19. supply; 20. scarcity; 21. profit

Bonus Page 139: 1.–2. Answers will vary.

Bonus Page 140: 1. Solar energy converted the salt water into freshwater through the process of evaporation.; 2. This process could be used on a larger scale in areas on Earth where there are low supplies of freshwater.

Bonus Page 141: 1.–5. Answers will vary.

Bonus Page 142: The following boxes should be colored: Christopher Columbus, Vasco da Gama, Samuel de Champlain, Juan Ponce de León, Sir Francis Drake, John Cabot, Marco Polo, Amerigo Vespucci, and Leif Eriksson.

Bonus Page 143: Answers will vary but may include 1. Michelangelo, Sofonisba Anguissola, Leonardo da Vinci; 2. Blaise Pascal, Isaac Newton, Nicolaus Copernicus; 3. William Shakespeare, Dante Alighieri, Geoffrey Chaucer; 4. Martin Luther, John Calvin, Thomas More; 5. Elizabeth I, Henry VII, Catherine de Medici; 6. Peter Henlein; Johannes Gutenberg, Galileo Galilei.

bio
(life)

© Carson Dellosa

derm
(skin)

© Carson Dellosa

prim
(first)

© Carson Dellosa

sci
(know)

© Carson Dellosa

sens/senti
(feel)

© Carson Dellosa

flex/flect
(bend)

© Carson Dellosa

cycl
(circular)

© Carson Dellosa

liter
(letter)

© Carson Dellosa

popul
(people)

© Carson Dellosa

primer
primitive
primary

© Carson Dellosa

epidermis
pachyderm
dermatologist

© Carson Dellosa

biology
biosphere
biography

© Carson Dellosa

reflex
flexible
reflection

© Carson Dellosa

sensitive
sentiment
sensory

© Carson Dellosa

scientist
conscious
omniscient

© Carson Dellosa

popular
population
repopulate

© Carson Dellosa

literary
literature
illiterate

© Carson Dellosa

cycle
cyclops
bicycle

© Carson Dellosa

vid/vis
(see)

chron
(time)

liber
(free)

© Carson Dellosa

© Carson Dellosa

© Carson Dellosa

study : student : :
teach : _____

hen : egg : :
sheep : _____

hungry : eat : :
thirsty : _____

© Carson Dellosa

© Carson Dellosa

© Carson Dellosa

wind : sailboat : :
gasoline : _____

piano : keys : :
guitar : _____

Illinois : state : :
Peru : _____

© Carson Dellosa

© Carson Dellosa

© Carson Dellosa

liberty
deliberate
liberal

© Carson Dellosa

synchronize
chronology
anachronism

© Carson Dellosa

video
invisible
envision

© Carson Dellosa

hungry : eat ::
thirsty : <u>drink</u>

© Carson Dellosa

hen : egg ::
sheep : <u>wool</u>

© Carson Dellosa

study : student ::
teach : <u>teacher</u>

© Carson Dellosa

Illinois : state ::
Peru : <u>country</u>

© Carson Dellosa

piano : keys ::
guitar : <u>strings</u>

© Carson Dellosa

wind : sailboat ::
gasoline : <u>car</u>

© Carson Dellosa

haul : hall ::
slay : _____

© Carson Dellosa

drab : colorful ::
dry : _____

© Carson Dellosa

mug : cup ::
saucer : _____

© Carson Dellosa

couch : cushion ::
bed : _____

© Carson Dellosa

positive : negative ::
least : _____

© Carson Dellosa

pointer : finger ::
molar : _____

© Carson Dellosa

blade : grass ::
drop : _____

© Carson Dellosa

flower : bouquet ::
page : _____

© Carson Dellosa

nails : clip ::
teeth : _____

© Carson Dellosa

mug : cup ::
saucer : _plate_

© Carson Dellosa

drab : colorful ::
dry : _wet_

© Carson Dellosa

haul : hall ::
slay : _sleigh_

© Carson Dellosa

pointer : finger ::
molar : _tooth_

© Carson Dellosa

positive : negative ::
least : _most_

© Carson Dellosa

couch : cushion ::
bed : _mattress_

© Carson Dellosa

nails : clip ::
teeth : _brush_

© Carson Dellosa

flower : bouquet ::
page : _book_

© Carson Dellosa

blade : grass ::
drop : _water_

© Carson Dellosa

carrot : rabbit : :
banana : _____

© Carson Dellosa

simile

© Carson Dellosa

metaphor

© Carson Dellosa

personification

© Carson Dellosa

idiom

© Carson Dellosa

allusion

© Carson Dellosa

$$\frac{5}{8} = \frac{x}{48}$$

© Carson Dellosa

$$\frac{5}{25} = \frac{x}{50}$$

© Carson Dellosa

$$\frac{6}{20} = \frac{x}{100}$$

© Carson Dellosa

The bungee jumper was a giant <u>yo-yo</u>, flying up and down through space.

© Carson Dellosa

The freshly mown lawn looked <u>like</u> <u>a green carpet</u> stretching to the street.

© Carson Dellosa

carrot : rabbit : :
banana : <u>monkey</u>

© Carson Dellosa

Don't stay out too late, or you might <u>turn into a pumpkin.</u>

© Carson Dellosa

Malcolm <u>ran out of</u> <u>steam</u> by the end of the race and finished in fourth place.

© Carson Dellosa

The wind <u>pushed</u> <u>through the open</u> <u>window and played</u> with the curtains.

© Carson Dellosa

$$\frac{6}{20} = \frac{30}{100}$$

© Carson Dellosa

$$\frac{5}{25} = \frac{10}{50}$$

© Carson Dellosa

$$\frac{5}{8} = \frac{30}{48}$$

© Carson Dellosa

$$\frac{3}{x} = \frac{42}{70}$$

© Carson Dellosa

$$\frac{9}{7} = \frac{45}{x}$$

© Carson Dellosa

$$\frac{x}{8} = \frac{3}{4}$$

© Carson Dellosa

$$\frac{4}{6} = \frac{x}{48}$$

© Carson Dellosa

$$\frac{x}{6} = \frac{55}{30}$$

© Carson Dellosa

$$13 + (-6) = \underline{\quad}$$

© Carson Dellosa

$$-9 - (-2) = \underline{\quad}$$

© Carson Dellosa

$$-5 + 3 = \underline{\quad}$$

© Carson Dellosa

$$8 - (-5) = \underline{\quad}$$

© Carson Dellosa

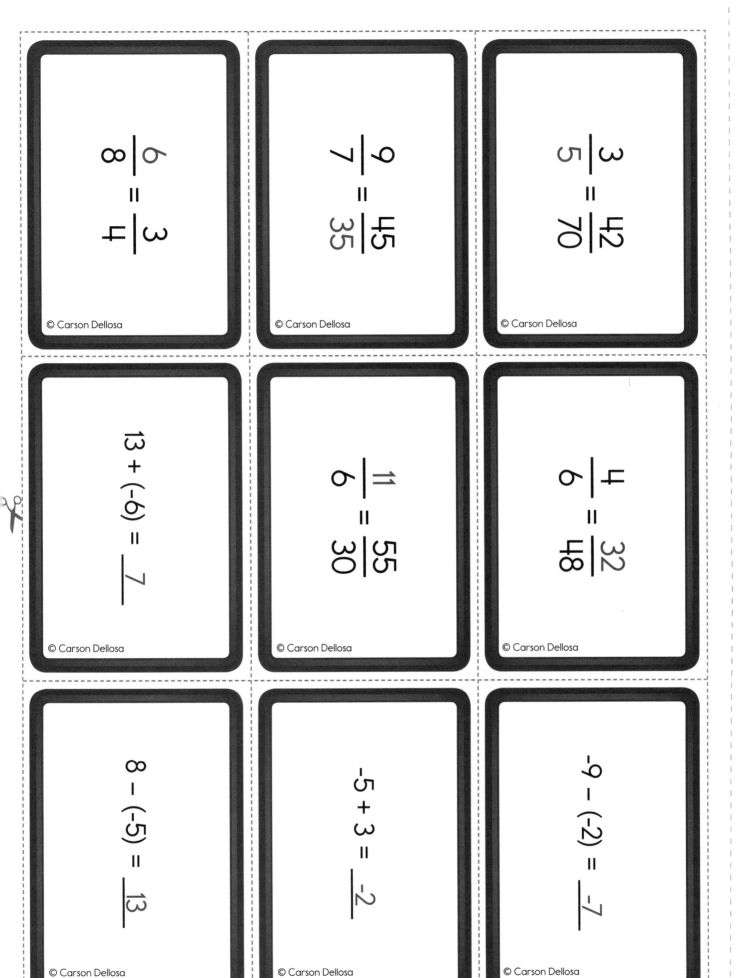

$$\frac{6}{8} = \frac{3}{4}$$

© Carson Dellosa

$$\frac{9}{7} = \frac{45}{35}$$

© Carson Dellosa

$$\frac{3}{5} = \frac{42}{70}$$

© Carson Dellosa

$$13 + (-6) = \underline{\ 7\ }$$

© Carson Dellosa

$$\frac{11}{6} = \frac{55}{30}$$

© Carson Dellosa

$$\frac{4}{6} = \frac{32}{48}$$

© Carson Dellosa

$$8 - (-5) = \underline{\ 13\ }$$

© Carson Dellosa

$$-5 + 3 = \underline{\ -2\ }$$

© Carson Dellosa

$$-9 - (-2) = \underline{\ -7\ }$$

© Carson Dellosa

-2 - 12 ___

15 - (-3) = ___

7 + (-11) = ___

-6 - (-9) = ___

5x ≥ 30

x + 3² = 17

8 + 2x < 14

x - 9 = 2³

7x - x ≤ 36

© Carson Dellosa

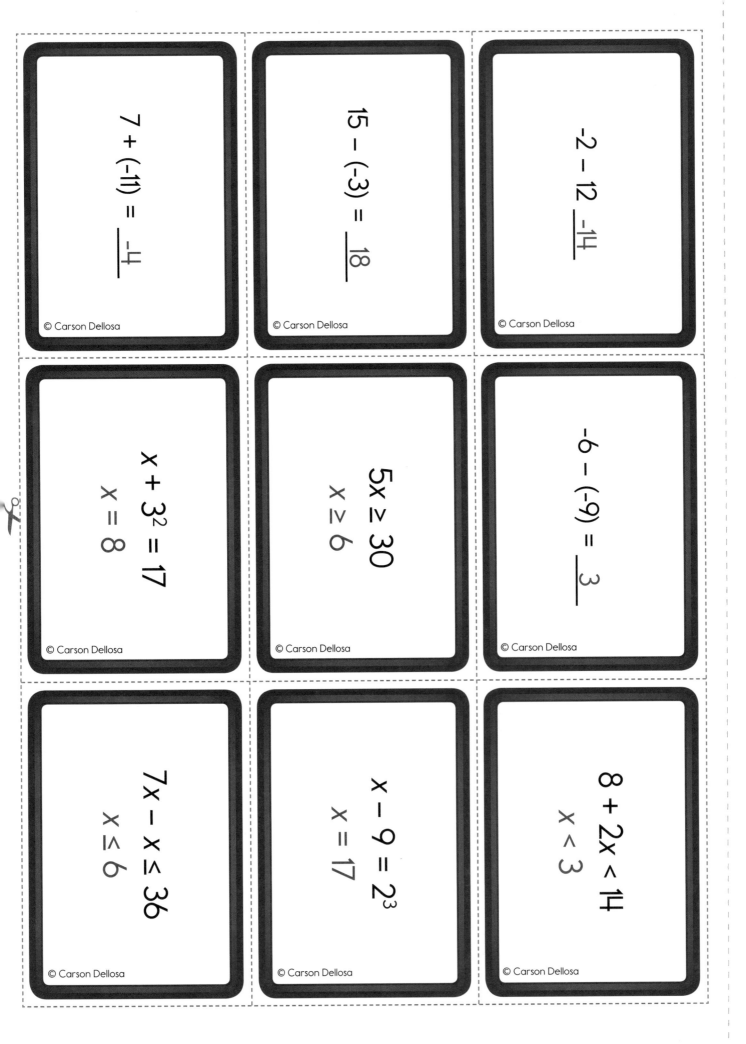

$-2 - 12$ __−14__

© Carson Dellosa

$15 - (-3) =$ __18__

© Carson Dellosa

$7 + (-11) =$ __−4__

© Carson Dellosa

$-6 - (-9) =$ __3__

© Carson Dellosa

$5x \geq 30$
$x \geq 6$

© Carson Dellosa

$x + 3^2 = 17$
$x = 8$

© Carson Dellosa

$8 + 2x < 14$
$x < 3$

© Carson Dellosa

$x - 9 = 2^3$
$x = 17$

© Carson Dellosa

$7x - x \leq 36$
$x \leq 6$

© Carson Dellosa

40 − 3x = x

x + x + x > 25 − 4

4x − 7 = 21

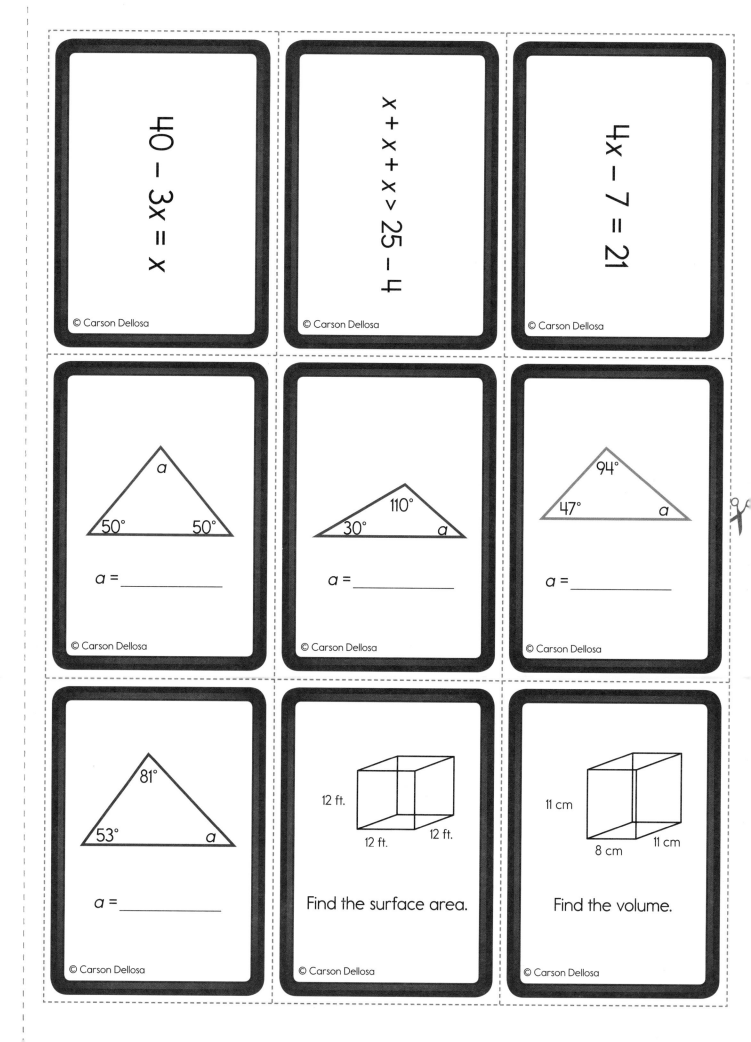

a = _____

50°   50°
a

a = _____

30°   110°   a

a = _____

94°
47°   a

a = _____

81°
53°   a

Find the surface area.

12 ft.
12 ft.   12 ft.

Find the volume.

11 cm
8 cm   11 cm

$4x - 7 = 21$
$x = 7$

© Carson Dellosa

$x + x + x > 25 - 4$
$x > 7$

© Carson Dellosa

$40 - 3x = x$
$x = 10$

© Carson Dellosa

$a = \underline{\quad 39° \quad}$

© Carson Dellosa

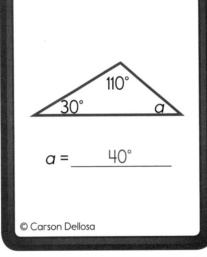

$a = \underline{\quad 40° \quad}$

© Carson Dellosa

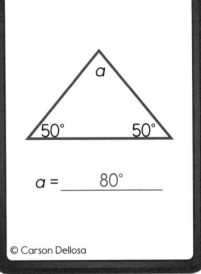

$a = \underline{\quad 80° \quad}$

© Carson Dellosa

Volume =
968 cubic cm

© Carson Dellosa

Surface area =
864 square feet

© Carson Dellosa

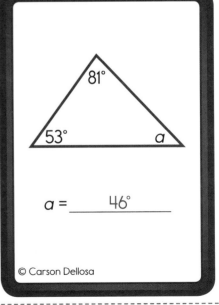

$a = \underline{\quad 46° \quad}$

© Carson Dellosa

SummerBridge
ACTIVITIES®

Congratulations!

This certifies that

_____
Name

has completed **Summer Bridge Activities.**

_____
Parent's Signature